THE BUTCHERS

Gareth Harris has cut his teeth as a writer with his weekly contributions to the Pontypridd match programme on the early history of the club. These features attracted much interest and admiration and encouraged him to offer his research for development as a book. A family man who has lived in the town all his life, he is continuing to devote all his spare time to beavering away in the public libraries and newspaper offices of South Wales to provide material for further volumes in the series.

Alan Evans was born and bred in Mid Glamorgan and after teaching in England for thirty years is now a full time rugby writer. Amongst his claims to fame is an unbroken run of watching 78 International Championship matches at Cardiff Arms Park. In this book he has related the achievements of the Pontypridd pioneers to the early development of the national game in Wales.

The Butchers Arms Boys

by

Gareth Harris
&
Alan Evans

Rugby Unlimited

First Published in Great Britain in October 1997
by Rugby Unlimited
61 Leonard Street, Neath, South Wales, SA11 3HW

© Rugby Unlimited 1997

British Library Cataloguing-in-publication Data

A catalogue record of this book is available from the British Library

ISBN 0 9531714 0 X

Designed and produced in Great Britain by Coveropen Ltd. Tel (01524 425478)

CONTENTS

ILLUSTRATIONS

Front cover illustration by Jonathan Evans

FOREWORD

by

PETER JOHNSON

of BBC Radio Wales

Gareth Harris is a brave man. He must be. Writing a history of a club called Pontypridd with a sticking *'P'* on your typewriter is a tough job. It requires patience and devotion to the task, qualities which Gareth has in abundance. I know about the typewriter key because for some years I have been editing Gareth's work for the Pontypridd match programme, in particular his popular column called "Looking Back". This column was the basis of the idea for this book, which we talked over two years ago.

Since then he has been hard at work, drawing together the threads of the early years of the club. Who would have thought that the outfit which takes winning in its stride these days was once more concerned about turning out enough players to give the opposition a game ?

The last quarter of the 19th century left a vivid mark on the South Wales landscape, architecture and politics changed forever. One feature of that age remains unaltered - the love of rugby football. Lloyd George didn't understand it. He thought the people of South Wales were affected by what he called "rampant footballism". Thankfully, they still are.

Gareth's research will ensure that all today's supporters get a taste of times past and a glimpse of some of the fascinating characters without whom there would be no cup run, no league win and no Ole, Ole, Ole !

PETER JOHNSON
Pontypridd
September 1997

INTRODUCTION (1)

It was not until the late 1870s that "football" first began to be reported, and even then, because Pontypridd's games were against public school teams, they rarely got mentioned. The first reports were brief and mostly appeared in the "Western Mail" and only then when they played in Cardiff.

Match reports are as far as possible reproduced in the style that they appeared in the newspapers of the time and therefore some words may appear strange today. "Chasing the leather" and other less obvious contemporary terminology are explained in the Footnote to the book. So, too, are the various scoring systems that developed in the 1880s as well as the team formations.

Some results and reports I have been unable to trace as often, especially towards the end of a season, results went unreported and many scheduled matches were not even played. Pontypridd, especially before 1880, rarely sent in match reports for home games to the "Western Mail" and most of the Pontypridd papers for the period are missing.

In my search for information, several people have been a great help. The staff of Cardiff Central Library and the Glamorgan Record Office, their counterparts in Rhondda-Cynon-Taff Library Services, and Mrs Penny Pugh and her colleagues at Pontypridd Library have often pointed me in the right direction. Other help came from Les Williams whose archive work and programme production at Llanelli RFC have long been admired. Nearer home there was David Davies of Pontypridd and Wayne Morgan. Within the family there was my mother who financed my research trips and my wife, Elaine, who put up with years of noisy typing. With some regret, I must also thank a certain Mrs. Thatcher for giving me lots of spare time.

I am indebted to Peter Johnson, an eminent broadcaster who never fails to extol the virtues of all things Pontypridd, for contributing the Foreword.

Finally, I must give special thanks to Dave Richards and Alan Evans and their exciting new venture at *Rugby Unlimited* for making a dream come true.

This book is dedicated to the men who carried the club through its early days - pioneers like James and William Spickett, Eddie and Ack Llewellyn, Teddy Lewis, John Daniel Jones and many others. I am sure they would be proud if they could see the success and fame that the club now enjoys. I can almost hear them shout their favourite motto, "Pontypridd to the fore !!"

"The Butchers Arms Boys" will hopefully be the first of a series of books that chart the history of the Pontypridd Rugby Football Club. I hope you will gain as much enjoyment from reading it as I have had with the research.

GARETH HARRIS
August 1997

INTRODUCTION (2)

Most rugby clubs have an inner core of loyal followers whose commitment to the cause is discernible in different ways. Some devote long hours to the running of the club, whether through committee work, the maintenance of the site, or the organisation of the clubhouse and bars. Others eschew formal responsibilities within the club's structure but enthusiastically support the team's performance on the field each week.

Gareth Harris is the bloke on the bob bank for every home game, but he is hardly typical. Gareth's club is Pontypridd, and his second home is their ground at Sardis Road. 'Ponty' is a club that is synonymous with a sense of belonging, that has grown from within, and which has a fervent level of support in the late 1990s. Anyone who saw the club's match programme during the championship-winning season of 1996-97 will have some awareness of Gareth Harris. The back page feature, 'Looking Back', was Gareth's weekly contribution to the cause. Throughout the season he recalled significant matches in the club's history. Such articles are not written easily. They require research and accuracy. In Gareth's case they also required days of cycling around the public libraries and local newspaper offices of South Wales.

At the end of Pontypridd's season of triumph, Gareth asked Dave Richards and myself at *Rugby Unlimited* to look at the results of his travels. What we saw was, to say the least, impressive. The early records of the Pontypridd club had long since been lost, though a centenary season had been celebrated in some style in 1976. As well as unearthing a rich vein of personalities and a somewhat fragmented pattern of match reports, Gareth discovered that the club may well have started up at least a year later than was generally believed.

It has been a pleasure to support this venture and to write an account that relates developments in Pontypridd in the late 19th century to the growth of rugby football in South Wales at that time.

Set in the days of the great coal boom in the Rhondda Valleys, this book tells of how a few young men from the county courthouse, who during their spare time played "football" in the local fields, gathered together with a few solicitors' clerks and sons of shop owners to form a town football club. They did so at a time when other clubs were being formed across South Wales, and within a short while fixtures were arranged and the legend that is Pontypridd Rugby Football Club was born.

ALAN EVANS
August 1997

CHAPTER 1

THE BEGINNING - JAMES SPICKETT AND THE FIRST MATCHES

"TO Welshmen, Pontypridd is a famous town and the gateway to some of the most important valleys in the history of coal production but it is difficult to assess accurately when rugby began to be played there".

The words are those of the late JBG Thomas, rugby journalist and historian and Pontypridd born and bred, in "The Illustrated History of Welsh Rugby", published in 1980. The Welsh Rugby Union celebrated its centenary that year, yet the landmark of the 100 years existence of the Pontypridd Rugby Football Club had already been reached four years before in 1976. The exact origins of the club that is today, simply, "Ponty" remain shrouded in some uncertainty. The records up to 1945 were destroyed in a fire, and even the excellent Centenary Brochure of 1976 acknowledges that "Pontypridd's beginnings are difficult to establish".

What we can be sure of is that a young articled clerk, James Spickett, whose father had come to the town from Cowbridge nearly 30 years before, was responsible in the late 1870s for establishing a town rugby team. Many years later, in a newspaper article dated 29th April 1926, Spickett gave an interview entitled "First Football in Wales". He told how he and Mr. Walter Morgan, the chief clerk at the County Courthouse in Pontypridd, decided to try and form a town rugby team. The club was born out of a meeting of colleagues and friends at the Butchers Arms in Taff Street.

James Spickett said in the article :

'Association was hardly dreamt of in those days, so our minds naturally turned to the amateur rugby code, and the result was that a club was formed and went strongly. We went to various places in South Wales, and it was interesting to notice many similar clubs sprang into existence at Aberdare, Merthyr and Llanelli.'

But when ?

Spickett gives no date for the first meeting, but he did become the first club captain. We know, too, that he was born in 1860 and as he says that he was 17 years old at the time of the meeting it is reasonable to assume that the earliest the club could have been formed was 1877. The earliest Pontypridd match reports do not appear until 1878, so it is also probable that the club's first season was 1877-78.

A further complication is that the 1926 newspaper report gives James Spickett's age as 68 rather than the 66 that records show that he would have been at the time. Was his memory failing him - or was it just a newspaper typing error ? The consequent inaccuracy in the report is the probable source of the previously accepted theory that Pontypridd Rugby Club was founded in 1875-76.

Whatever the exact date, what is beyond doubt is that the decade of the 1870s was a time when rugby football clubs were being established throughout South Wales in general and the mining valleys in particular. The town of Pontypridd was ripe for the development of organised sport. From the mid 1860s it had rapidly grown into a large coal and railway town with professional men arriving from other areas. One such arrival was Mr Edward Collett Spickett of Cowbridge, the new Superintendent Registrar for Pontypridd and eventual father of two rugby-playing sons, James and William Spickett.

The growth of the population was indeed rapid. Between 1871 and 1881, it increased in Pontypridd from 51,000 to 93,000 and this placed heavy demands on environmental health and social conditions. Housing standards were very poor, with damp, overcrowded dwellings, filthy privvies and a water supply liable to faecal pollution. Slaughter houses, dairies and common lodging houses were unregulated and with two

JAMES SPICKETT
Founder member of Pontypridd Rugby Football Club and club captain in 1877-78 and again in 1882-83. James later developed a distinguished career in the law, becoming Registrar of the County Court held at Pontypridd, Ystradfodwg, and Porth and Clerk to the Pontypridd Burial Board.

[Photograph courtesy Rhondda, Cynon, Taff Library Service]

WALTER MORGAN
The Chief Clerk at the County Courthouse who, as a young man, met with James Spickett to plan a town rugby team. Another who went on to a distinguished professional career, becoming an Under Sheriff for Glamorgan and an Alderman and Vice-Chairman of the Glamorgan County Council.

dirty rivers running through the centre of town the health of the majority of the people was constantly at risk. Cases of croup and severe sore throat were common place. However, the landed gentry and the well-educated were less at risk from these ailments. Throughout South Wales former students of public schools such as that at Monmouth were instrumental in setting up the new rugby clubs. The club at Pontypridd was formed by lads from professional families who fell into the well-educated category, were better off than most, and who escaped the worst ravages of the poor living conditions in several parts of the town.

The probable formation of Pontypridd Rugby Football Club in 1877 also fits in with organisational changes elsewhere in the South Wales clubs . The first, and therefore senior, Welsh club was established at Neath in 1871. Others soon followed in Llanelli, Swansea, Newport and Cardiff. Then in 1875 a South Wales Football Club had been formed in Brecon. This was a change of direction. This was to be a team of all the talents, comprised of the leading players from the South Wales clubs, that would be strong enough to compete with the more experienced English clubs. The SWFC did indeed achieve some success on the field of play but within three years the approach had changed again. In 1878, the *Club* was replaced by the *Union :* clubs, rather than players, would belong to the South Wales Football Union.

During its short existence, the South Wales Football Club had inaugurated a competition for the South Wales Challenge Cup. In September 1877, the new club at Pontypridd was not one of the 18 clubs that paid the subscription of two guineas to compete in the knock-out competition, but two years later they were hopeful of inclusion. Unfortunately, when the draw was made at Cardiff on September 24th, 1879, no Pontypridd representative was present and as the entry fee had not been paid the club did not go into the first round draw.

Other matches were, thankfully, taking place. With the Taff Vale and Great Western Railways running through Pontypridd, initial fixtures were mostly arranged against teams whose grounds were accessible by train. Therefore, games against clubs from Cardiff (including Cardiff Banks and Monkton House School), Merthyr and Aberdare figured prominently. Match reports, mostly rather brief, began to appear in the "Western Mail".

It is reasonable to assume that James Spickett was the first captain, and the available match reports for 1878-79 show that by then the captaincy had passed to Henry Briscoe. He and his brother Phillip played in the same team as the illustrious Spickett brothers - James and William. Unlike others at the time, the Briscoes were neither solicitors' clerks or employees of the county courthouse. Nevertheless, they were from a well-to-do family. The 1881 Census shows a Henry Briscoe living at Typicca House, Hopkinstown. He was the general manager and part owner of the Great Western Colliery and was probably the father of Henry (junior) and Phillip. The "Henry" listed as Pontypridd captain would have been around 17 years of age. The brothers are not listed in the Census. It was possible that they were at the residential Cowbridge Grammar School, or even Monkton House School in Cardiff, both of which were hotbeds of "football" at the time.

The Spicketts and the Briscoes were to play in a series of games between October 1878 and October 1879 which were the first recorded in the pages of the newspapers of the time.

WILLIAM SPICKETT
The younger brother of James and, after a spell playing for Cardiff, captain of the Pontypridd club in 1883-84. A Liberal politician whose own propaganda once described him as "free from sectarian jealousy, the disease that saps the vitals of some of our best men" !!

17

THE FIRST REPORTED MATCHES

1878 - 1879

24th October 1878 - ABERDARE v. PONTYPRIDD

"The match was played under adverse circumstances, the weather being terrible and the players for a great proportion of the game were immersed in the water that literally covered the field. When halftime was called, the visitors held a slight advantage, but though at the finish the home side were in advance, no points had been scored. The match, which was very closely contested throughout, ended in a draw."

Match Drawn

The Pontypridd captain, Henry Briscoe, was unhappy before the game and complained to Prosser, the Aberdare captain, about the inclusion of T.B.Jones of Abergavenny and Osgood and Phillips of Merthyr in the home team. This led to some bitterness between the two clubs. Letters were sent to the "Western Mail" and in the issue of 26th October Mr Reynolds, the Aberdare secretary wrote that Messrs Phillips and Osgood were both residents of Aberdare and that Mr Jones had been a member of the Aberdare club for three years.

26th October 1878 - PONTYPRIDD v. MONKTON HOUSE SCHOOL

Team : Back : J.Lewis; Quarterbacks : Jenkins, Chittenden, J.Spickett, A.N.Other; Halves : Morris and Richards; Forwards : H.Briscoe (captain), Williams, Verity, Jones, W.Spickett, P.Briscoe and Roderick.

"At the commencement of the game the school had to act on the defensive, and E.R.Chittenden, the Pontypridd quarterback, got hold of the ball, and, by a good drop kick, sent it over the school bar. After halftime, however, the school played well up and more than once carried the ball into dangerous proximity to their opponents goal; but they could not succeed in carrying it across the line. The forward play on both sides was very good; Mr Forrester, of Merthyr, being a tower of strength for the Pontypridd team. For the school, E.J.Evans (captain), Anning and Caneva, distinguished themselves, especially by their collaring. Of the Pontypridd team, William Spickett and Williams played well. At the close of the game Pontypridd had scored 1 goal and 4 touchdowns to Monkton House School 0. The school team played one man short."

Pontypridd 1 Goal and 4 Touchdowns; Monkton House School 0

2nd November 1878 - MONKTON HOUSE SCHOOL v. CARDIFF SECONDS

A good example of players appearing for more than one team at the time. A week after playing against Monkton House School, James Spickett and E.R.Chittenden played *for* them at Sophia Gardens against Cardiff Seconds. Both players were attending the school at the time, or had just left.

7th November 1878 - CARDIFF BANKS v. PONTYPRIDD

Five days later, Spickett and Chittenden were on the field at Sophia Gardens again and back in their Pontypridd colours. This is the confusing fixture which still appears in Cardiff's records as a match played by their First XV against Pontypridd, but was in fact the team of Cardiff Banks.

Pontypridd Team : *Back : G.Williams; Quarterbacks : E.R.Chittenden and W.Jenkins; Halves : Spickett and Morris; Forwards : H.Briscoe (captain), G.R.Williams, W.S.Davies, E.Jenkins, W.Thomas, P.Briscoe, C.Verity; Richards (flying man).* [Note - 13 players]

"This match was played on Sophia Gardens field, Cardiff, each team turning out two men short of the usual number. Up to halftime the game was very even, neither side scoring, and each having to touch down once in self defence. About ten minutes before time, Sewell obtained a try for the bankers but the place kick did not result in a goal. The ball was touched down by Pontypridd in self defence, and shortly afterwards no-side was called, the visitors thus being defeated by 1 Try and 1 Touchdown to 1 Touchdown. Chittenden and Spickett were the most conspicuous for Pontypridd. Amongst the visitors' forwards, the play of Davies and Briscoe, and the running of Morris, deserve a special mention. It is only to be regretted that play was not commenced earlier. The ball being kicked-off at 4 o'clock, darkness setting on 'ere halftime was called. Mr Jones and Mr Thomas acted as umpires."

Cardiff Banks 1 Try and 1 Touchdown; Pontypridd 1 Touchdown

30th November 1878 - PONTYPRIDD v. 10th GLAMORGANSHIRE RIFLE VOLUNTEERS

Team : *Goal : Treharne; Halves : G.Williams, Dalziel; Quarterbacks : Morris and Chittenden; Forwards : W.Spickett, J.Spickett, Thomas, P.Briscoe, H.Briscoe (capt)*

The match, although played on a Saturday, saw Pontypridd play no less than five men short. This will explain some of the revised positions, such as 'Goal' instead of 'Back'. It was almost a case of the Spicketts, Briscoes and friends !

Pontypridd 1 Goal and 1 Try; GRV 3 Rouges

1879 - 1880

16th October 1879 - PONTYPRIDD v. COWBRIDGE GRAMMAR SCHOOL

This was the only match reported that season, and briefly at that. It was played on a Thursday and "after a severe struggle, the homesters emerged victors..."

Pontypridd 1 Try and 3 Touchdowns; Cowbridge Grammar School 0

It is possible that the fortunes of the Pontypridd club were reported under another name. Around 1880, the "Western Mail" started reporting games between Cardiff and Rhondda Valley, or Cardiff and Rhondda

United. A little later, C.S.Arthur's "History and Statistics" of the Cardiff club published in 1906 lists a match being played at home against "United Valleys (Rhondda)" on 1st January 1881.

Who were these teams ?

It appears that they were probably Pontypridd sides. There were no properly constituted teams in the Rhondda at the time (though, again, C.S.Arthur records Cardiff playing "E.Thomas' Team (Rhondda)" on 18th January 1879). Several Pontypridd players such as David and Edward Treharne and Tom Williams lived in the Rhondda and the club may have been fielding teams under other names to attract players down the valley. Indeed, the Rhondda players in the side may even have been trying to alter the name of the club !

The earliest record we have of Pontypridd playing a Rhondda side is during the 1886-87 season when Pontypridd played Pentre. As Pentre was the home village of David and Edward Treharne, perhaps it was Pontypridd that had helped sow the seeds of rugby in the Rhondda Valley.

CHAPTER 2

1880-81 - EDWARD TREHARNE AND A MOMENTOUS SEASON

WHENEVER James Spickett and his friends started the Pontypridd Rugby Football Club, whether it was 1876 or 1877, they could not have foreseen that within three or four short years their brainchild would be both celebrating and contributing towards several landmarks in the game.

On 19th February 1881, the name of Edward Llewellyn Treharne, a nineteen-years' old medical student from Cowbridge Grammar School, entered the annals of Pontypridd, national and international rugby. On that day at Mr Richardson's Field in Blackheath, London, the first ever Welsh XV played an international match against England. Treharne, a threequarter and half-back for the Pontypridd club, represented Wales - as a forward. It was a day when Wales suffered a very heavy defeat, but it was another staging post in the hectic twelve-months' period that saw the birth of the Welsh Rugby Union. The Pontypridd club figured prominently in the story.

The uncertainty about the exact date of the establishment of the club at Pontypridd is mirrored by the controversy over the exact origins of the Welsh Rugby Union. Was the national body set up in March 1880 or March 1881 ? If it was the former, then Pontypridd RFC is a founder club; if the latter, then it is not. Whatever, the club did have a player (and nearly two) in the first national XV.

It is generally accepted that a meeting of club representatives, convened by Richard Mullock of Newport, took place at the Tenby Hotel, Swansea, in March 1880. It is also accepted that the clubs represented were Cardiff, Chepstow, Haverfordwest, Llandaff, Llanelli,

Neath, Newport, Swansea - and Pontypridd. It seems likely that the formation of a national union was discussed, if only because Mullock was anxious to arrange an international fixture against England, but the perceived wisdom now is that the official inauguration was delayed for twelve months. On Saturday 12th March 1881, the Welsh Football Union was established at a meeting at the Castle Hotel, Neath. Eleven Welsh clubs were represented at the meeting. Pontypridd was not one of them. By then, however, Wales had already played its first international - and Pontypridd had been well represented in the shape of Edward Treharne.

Treharne's background was typical of so many of his era. Born in Merthyr in 1862, he received the then traditional middle-class education at Cowbridge Grammar School, already established as something of a rugby nursery for Pontypridd and other clubs, before becoming a medical student at St Bartholomew's Hospital in London. The match records available suggest that Edward may not have figured as prominently as his brother David in Pontypridd teams of the time. Indeed, in 1880-81 David Treharne continued a line begun by James Spickett and Henry Briscoe and was club captain. He it was who brought his brother down to Pontypridd from the family home in Pentre, Rhondda. In the following two seasons Edward Treharne was to appear in Cardiff colours (alongside William Spickett) but what is beyond doubt is that he was officially listed as "E.Treharne (Pontypridd)" in the team photograph for the first ever Welsh XV in 1881.

The match itself may have been somewhat lacking in the glamour or even organisation of international rugby a hundred years later. A victim of the latter may have been a certain J.E.Brooks who was one of two players who failed to arrive for their first caps. If he had turned up, John Edward Brooks' name would be alongside that of Edward Treharne's on Pontypridd's honours board. As it is, the unfortunate Brooks' explanation is well-documented in the Welsh Rugby Union's official history, "Fields of Praise" (Smith and Williams, 1981) :

'There was no organisation or committee assisting in 1880 to select players. All that would happen was that some individual would have a conversation with you, take your name and address,and pass on. That

happened to me after I had played for Pontypridd against Shewbrook's School at Sophia Gardens, Cardiff. It was mentioned to me that Treharne and I had been chosen to play for Wales against England in that first international. I had no definite instructions from anyone to play in that match, but I heard afterwards that I had been expected to play.'

Brooks never did play for Wales. He may never have been selected in the first place if more players had been available. Despite Richard Mullock's best efforts, the Rugby Football Union insisted, after a postponement on 22nd January, on 19th February as the date for the international. It was, they said, the only vacant date on their calendar. This coincided with a cup semi-final between Swansea and Llanelli. As a result, the only West Walian in the team was R.H.B.Summers of Haverfordwest. It was Summers who in later years further illustrated the confusion of that first international :

'We changed at a small old-fashioned inn nearby. When we got to our changing room, we discovered that we were two men short, their invitation apparently having gone astray. However, we picked up two varsity men with Welsh qualifications, and they agreed to fill the vacancies on condition that they were allowed to play threequarter......'

So it was that the speedy Edward Treharne joined the Welsh pack of nine forwards against the heavier and more powerful English pack of ten. The six Welsh backs hardly mattered against their five English counterparts as the home side, already the veterans of 18 previous international matches, triumphed by eight goals and six tries to nil. Treharne was to win one further cap, also against England the following January, but in the more accustomed position of half-back.

In the meantime, Summers' final words were more encouraging :

'...Despite the odds, we never gave up trying and at dinner that night Lenny Stokes, the England captain said : "We have seen enough to know that you Welshmen will be hard to beat in a few years time when you get together." '

Whatever the disappointments of Treharne and the first international match, his home club continued to make notable progress with its own fixtures. Before Christmas of 1880, Pontypridd had twice beaten Aberdare

EDWARD TREHARNE

Edward Llewellyn Treharne was Pontypridd's first 'cap'. A product of Cowbridge Grammar School and St Bartholomew's Hospital, his later life was spent in Barry where he was a freemason and district councillor. He died in 1904 at the age of 42.

THE FIRST WELSH XV 1881

The pioneers of the national team that lost to England at Mr Richardson's Field, Blackheath, in February 1881. Edward Treharne is the 'man in white' in the back row. The captain was James Alfred Bevan. It was his only 'cap' though he went on to have 13 children.

and also Bridgend in home matches. And on 4th November 1880, the club began its first great adventure in the South Wales Challenge Cup, an adventure which as in modern times was to lead to Cardiff Arms Park.

As the early rounds were played on neutral grounds, the Cup trail in fact began at the Arms Park against the Newport based club of Maindee. Pontypridd included in their XV the two Spicketts and David, but not Edward, Treharne. A significant, if narrow, victory was well-reported at the time, unlike the second round win over Newport Crusaders. Pontypridd then returned to the Arms Park on 12th February 1881 - one week before the inaugural international match - for what was in effect the "Eastern Final" of the cup. The western section was in some disarray with Neath and Swansea refusing to play each other.

The records of the Cardiff Rugby Club show that they had played and beaten Pontypridd on 7th November 1878. This originates from the mistaken report in the "Western Mail" which should have been "Cardiff Banks v. Pontypridd". Successive Cardiff histories from the highly-regarded book of C.S.Arthur in 1907 to the publications of D.E.Davies and Harris in recent years have missed a letter from the Cardiff secretary, J.A.Jones, informing the "Western Mail" a few days after the match that Pontypridd had played Cardiff Banks and not Cardiff RFC. The cup match of 1881 was therefore the first meeting of the two sides and a major landmark in the development of the Pontypridd club. That the match was lost hardly matters, for the Cardiff club was already a giant in the game and a month later was to win the cup itself after a titanic struggle with Llanelli in the final at Neath.

In his newspaper interview of 1926, James Spickett, whilst reproaching himself for the defeat, tacitly admits that the cup match was a beneficial experience :

'A curious thing is that in the contest with Newport Crusaders I put on the winning score just before the final whistle, but in the final I was somewhat the cause of bringing defeat on my side in Cardiff. In the Newport encounter I landed a beautiful drop-goal from midfield, owing to a sudden decision, as I was thinking of running a Try, but against Cardiff I had an unsuccessful struggle with Percy Head, who was looked

upon as one of the smartest players in Wales. I was acting as Fullback, though my usual position was at Halfback. The grim tackle took place in a pool of water in front of the posts. I caught the legs of my antagonist, but could not retain my grip.'

As with Edward Treharne in the international match, Spickett was experiencing the difficulties of playing out of position at the highest level. "Head" was in fact P.K.Heard who played 25 matches in four seasons for Cardiff. Pontypridd could only benefit from playing such illustrious opposition. They emerged with credit from a tough encounter. It was unfortunate that "football" was still a minority sport, and the Pontypridd players received little acclaim in their own town.

Eight of the Pontypridd XV had also played for Rhondda Valley against Cardiff on New Year's Day of 1881. In more recent times, the Pontypridd club has hosted matches such as Cardiff v Mid-District XV, the latter team including players from the modern day Merthyr, Treorchy, Senghenydd, Cilfynydd and other clubs alongside their Pontypridd colleagues. In 1881, it was another innovation in what was truly a momentous season for Pontypridd.

THE CLUB MATCHES OF 1880-1881

Three home matches were comprehensively reported in the late autumn of 1880. That all three should result in clear victories suggests an encouraging advance by the club. The reports create vivid images of well-contested "scrimmages", last ditch defence, and enthusiastic (and apparently prodigious !) kicking. Also emerging are the personalities, if not star players, of the time with George Williams taking his place alongside the Spicketts and Treharne as an influential presence.

28th October 1880 - PONTYPRIDD v. ABERDARE

A match that took place on a Thursday afternoon.

"The ball was kicked off by the visitors, and returned immediately to their 25 where a determined scrimmage took place, and from this place, and from this time until the end of the game, it was invariably kept in their territory. The match therefore was wholly in favour of the home team which on this occasion was by no means a representative one. The points scored were, Pontypridd 1 Goal and 2 Tries, Aberdare 0. Had it not been for the rain that poured down incessantly throughout the afternoon and rendered the ball most difficult to handle, the Pontypriddians would no doubt have doubled their score. The Pontypridd Tries were scored by Treharne and W.Spickett."

Pontypridd 1 Goal and 2 Tries; Aberdare 0

13th November 1880 - PONTYPRIDD v. BRIDGEND

"Bridgend visited Pontypridd in very wet weather, and the match resulted in favour of the home team by a Goal and a few Touchdowns to a disputed Try.

Owing to a breakdown accident on the way, the Bridgend team did not arrive until 3.45, and by this time the Pontypridd team had gone home. Nevertheless, the Pontypriddians managed to get together fourteen men.

The Pontypridd captain having won the toss, chose to play with a slight wind blowing in their favour. Bridgend kicked off, but the ball was returned by George Williams (Back). A scrimmage took place in the centre of the ground, and Bridgend, owing to their weight, took the ball into the home half, but a good kick from James Spickett sent the oval back to neutral ground. A scrimmage took place, and Parry, getting hold of the ball, passed to Brown, who by a splendid run took the ball close to the visitors' line, but was knocked into touch. The ball was thrown out and secured by Finch (Pontypridd), who obtained a Try. The place kick was entrusted to George Williams, who kicked a splendid goal. Halftime was then called.

By this time it was getting almost too dark for the players to see the ball. By a splendid drop from Verity, the ball was sent from the visitors' 25 to the home territory, and the Bridgend men following up hard, almost secured a Try. A scrimmage was formed nearly on the Pontypridd line, and as the ball was picked up in the scrimmage by one of the visiting forwards, the Try they claimed was disputed."

Pontypridd 1 Goal and a few Touchdowns; Bridgend 1 disputed Try

9th December 1880 - PONTYPRIDD v. ABERDARE

Team : Back : George Williams; Threequarters : D.Treharne (captain), J.D.Jones; Halves : James Spickett and William Spickett; Forwards : Williams, Parry, Lewis, C.Matthews, D.Jenkins, J.Richards, John, and Harris.

"This second home game of the season against Aberdare was played in excellent weather . The home team won the toss and let the visitors start the ball. It was well returned by George Williams, who by a long drop sent the leather deep into the visitors' territory, and through the good combined play of the home forwards, the ball was forced over the Aberdare goal-line to secure a Minor. As soon as the ball was kicked out from the 25 flag, James Spickett secured it, and made a good attempt at the visitors' goal, but was collared just in time by Davies. A scrimmage took place close to the visitors' goal-line, and had the home forwards played loose scrimmages at this point, their backs would undoubtedly have scored a Try, but the Aberdarians managed to touch down in self defence. Halftime was then called.

Early in the second half, Pontypridd scored another Touchdown. The ball being restarted, was secured by Treharne, who by a good run, and dodging all his opponents, obtained a Try, but the kick for goal was unsuccessful. Again the leather was set in motion, and under the custody of William Spickett, who made a good run, was knocked into touch a few yards from the Aberdare goal-line. A drop from one of the visitors sent the ball into neutral territory, but was secured by Treharne, who dropped a splendid goal. Nothing of note occured after this, except the visitors were compelled to touchdown in defence a few times. When full time was called the score stood as follows ......"

Pontypridd 1 Goal, 1 Try and 6 Touchdowns; Aberdare 0

A FIRST CUP RUN

Having successfully entered the competition for the South Wales Challenge Cup in 1880-81, the club set about negotiating the early rounds before Christmas. The competition was played in two sections, East and West Wales, with the winners of each section playing in a grand final. It was a great fillip to Pontypridd, their players and their supporters, that at this first attempt they were to go all the way to the East Wales Final at Cardiff Arms Park.

Indeed, Pontypridd's very first cup match was against the Newport club, Maindee, at a neutral Cardiff Arms Park on a fine Thursday afternoon in early November. It was to feature all the traditional cut-and-thrust of cup football and no little controversy.

4th November 1880 - MAINDEE v. PONTYPRIDD

South Wales Challenge Cup - Round 1

Team : *Back : George Williams; Threequarters : D.Treharne (captain), J.Spickett, J.D.Jones; Halves : W.Spickett and E.Williams; Forwards :*

G.R.Williams, Lewis, John, Parry, Richards, Jenkins, Matthews, Harris, and Matthews.

"The Newport men won the toss and elected to play with the sun at their backs, and at 3.30 the ball was kicked off by the Pontypridd side. It was well returned by Maindee, and being backed up in fine style, the following play went on well inside the Pontypridd 25. A Try was very soon secured by Maindee, but went unconverted, but owing to bad play on the part of Pontypridd, they lost another point directly afterwards. On the ball being kicked for goal, it was neatly seized and touched down for Maindee by L.Williams, which secured another Try for them. McDaniel kicked, but no goal resulted.

After a Touchdown had been added to Maindee's score, the ball got into neutral ground, but here a couple of Maindee men showed bad form by missing the leather, which went consequently to the foot of a Pontypridd man, and a Try was scored by Parry. This was, however, not converted into a goal, the kick only making a 'Poster'. Soon after this point had been placed to the credit of Pontypridd, a run was made by William Spickett, which resulted in another Try for them. George Williams kicked, but no goal resulted.

Soon after halftime, the Maindee men secured a Try, which McDaniel failed to convert into a goal. After this point in the game, the play gave the Maindee men great dissatisfaction. It happened thus : The ball was averred, kicked out of the scrimmage into touch, and was then taken on by Treharne, when it should, of course, have been again submitted to a scrimmage. As it was however, Treharne ran for goal and secured a first class Try, which was allowed by the umpires, and was converted by George Williams. Time was called immediately afterwards, and the game resulted in a win for Pontypridd by 2 Goals, 1 Try, and 1 Touchdown, to 4 Tries and 3 Touchdowns, or by one point."

Pontypridd 2 Goals, 1 Try and 1 Touchdown; Maindee 4 Tries and 3 Touchdowns

Pontypridd went on to defeat **NEWPORT CRUSADERS** in the Second Round in a match that apparently received little press coverage.

The Third Round match, which was effectively the East Wales Final, at Cardiff Arms Park was the biggest game in the Pontypridd club's short history. It turned into something of a match of rearguard action and honourable defeat. Both the Spickett brothers played out of position against a team that were destined to win the Cup Final against Llanelli four weeks later.

12th February 1881 - CARDIFF v. PONTYPRIDD
South Wales Challenge Cup - Round 3

Team : *Back : J.Spickett, G.Williams; Threequarters : D.Treharne (captain), E.D.Williams; Halves : Branfil, E.Treharne, F.Davies; Forwards : G.R.Williams, W.Spickett, Lewis, Parry, Matthews, Wrayer, Richards, Rees.*

"The Cardiff Arms Park was soft and slippery, but not withstanding this, a rough and exciting game passed off with but a few mishaps. There was a large number of spectators on the ground, the cause being probably the importance attached to the issue of the game, or the fact of it being the first game played in the town for many weeks, bringing a return of its novelty.

The game was opened by Spickett kicking off for Pontypridd, and though it stuck for a time in the Cardiff quarters, it was soon kicked out from that locality further afield, and soon afterwards went across the ground with a rush, the ultimate result of which was a touchdown in favour of Cardiff. This was rapidly followed by a bit of good play by Hybart in the Pontypridd 25, which took the ball through the Pontypridd forwards and into the hands of Head, who made a plucky run and touched down in a fairly good place just as he was about to be collared by a couple of Pontypriddians.

A good kick was made, which resulted, however, in nothing, and the ball was again kicked off. The ball had not long been moving, however, before almost the same thing occurred once more, Percy Head - a regular flying man - getting the leather and making a Try at a more difficult angle than before.

Sewell again took the kick in hand, but made a bad attempt. The next Try scored by Cardiff was got by Evans, and Sewell's kick again proved of no effect.

Nothing more of importance transpired before halftime was given out.

The second half of the game, the teams of course having changed sides, was a regular history of attempts on the part of Pontypridd to make the best of a losing game by frequent touchdowns in defence, and it was not before at least half-a- dozen of these were scored that time was called. Both sides had made strenuous efforts to secure a more decided point in the game, but these, as we have said, did not result in any, and at the call of time, after a rough and tumble game, in which both sides played well, the score stood at a win for Cardiff by 3 Tries and a number of Touchdowns, to 0."

Cardiff 3 Tries and Touchdowns; Pontypridd 0

AN EARLY HOLIDAY FIXTURE

In the early years of their own history, Cardiff began to play what could be called Combined XVs from their neighbouring smaller clubs. One of the earliest was on New Year's Day, 1881, against a Rhondda Valley team. The Cardiff club's records list their opponents as United Valleys (Rhondda). Several of the Pontypridd players appear in the combined team which was led by David Treharne. The report highlights two issues of the age - turning up on time and having enough players !

1st January 1881 - CARDIFF v. RHONDDA VALLEY

Rhondda Team : Backs : G.Williams and J.Spickett; Threequarters : Lewis and E. Treharne; Halves : E.D.Williams and D.Treharne (captain); Forwards : R.Lewis, G.R. Williams, E.Rees, D.Jenkins, E.Williams, J.Price, J.D.Jones.

"This match on New Year's Day 1881 was played on a very soft and slippery Cardiff Arms Park, and no runs were made during the game. The Rhondda team, which was taken from the lower part of the valley, from Pentre down, but for the most part from Pontypridd, played 2 men short, but turned up on time. The result was a victory for Cardiff....The Rhondda men had shown a great improvement in form, and had played well together."

Cardiff 1 Try and 6 Touchdowns; Rhondda Valley 1 Touchdown

CHAPTER 3

1881-85 - TOM WILLIAMS AND THE YEARS OF CONSOLIDATION

THE story of rugby in Wales since the 1870s is enriched with characters who through their ability, selfless devotion to the game, and sheer hard work have left a lasting imprint on its history. Such a person was Thomas Williams (Llwynypia) - another fond Welsh idiosyncrasy is to append a hometown or birthplace to the hero's name.

Tom Williams was Pontypridd's second international player and he was a great deal more as well : official, administrator both within Wales and beyond, international referee and even a touch judge. His playing career coincided with the further advance of the Pontypridd club amongst the South Wales rugby fraternity and his years of officialdom culminated in his presence at probably the greatest day of all - Wales 3, New Zealand nil in 1905. Look at the Welsh team photograph for that historic achievement and you will see Williams standing alongside J.F.Williams in the back row.

Tom Williams was born at Llwynypia Farm, Llwynypia in the Rhondda Valley and spent his early days living in the Tonypandy Inn. His training as a solicitor was in Pontypridd, probably at Spickett's Solicitors in Gelliwasted Road. His cap came as a member of the Welsh pack against Ireland at Lansdowne Road on 28th January 1882. This was Wales' second international match - so following Edward Treharne's appearance against England eleven months' earlier the Pontypridd club had representatives in the first two Welsh XV's. The match in Dublin was also Wales' first international victory. It was, though, an unhappy match. Two Irish players left the field in protest at the refereeing of the Welsh official, Richard Mullock, and two more were injured, leaving the home side with eleven players. Wales won comfortably by two goals and two tries to nil.

Inevitably, perhaps, other clubs had designs on Tom Williams' playing ability. The Cardiff records claim him as one of theirs at the time of his cap. He had played for them in their cup final against Llanelli at the end of the previous season and was eventually to play in their colours 53 times over a period of seven seasons. At the time, it was not unusual for players to turn out for other clubs when their regular side did not have a game. But in January 1882 Tom Williams was a member of the Pontypridd club and the official WRU records for the Irish match confirm him as such. To his credit his playing career turned full circle and ended in his birthplace : he became a leading light in the founding of the team at Llwynypia.

A second career beckoned for Tom Williams. He became a referee and appears in several Welsh team photographs as the touch judge. He refereed at least three Barbarians' matches in South Wales against Newport and Cardiff before officiating at the England v. Ireland international match at the Rectory Field, Blackheath, on 13th February, 1904. During the same period, Williams did much good work and was a well-loved figure off the field. In 1884 he had become the first secretary of the Rhondda, Ferndale and Aberdare League - the Glamorgan League of later years - and then represented Mid-District on the Welsh Rugby Union from 1899 to 1910. He was also a national selector and, from 1901 until 1908, a Welsh representative on the International Board.

Tom Williams' final claim to fame surrounds the great Welsh victory over the 1905 All Blacks. He was the uncle of W.M.(Willie) Llewellyn of Penygraig, the Welsh wing that day. It was Williams who suggested that the Welsh players should sing the Welsh National Anthem *after* the Maori War Song prior to kick-off. This they did. Another great Welsh tradition was born.

By 1908, Tom Williams had withdrawn from active participation in rugby administration. He lived on for five more years, but as an invalid. His keen enthusiasm for Wales and its prowess in all games was patriotically sustained to the last days of his life. The Saturday before he

October 15, 1881

LOCAL & DISTRICT INTELLIGENCE.

FOOT BALL CLUB.—A concert in aid of the above named club was held at the Market Hall, on Wednesday evening, in which the following ladies and gentlemen took part :—Mdme. S. A. Williams, Miss Julia Thomas, Miss James, Dr. Dickson, Mr Tom Morgan, Mr D. Bowen, Mr F. Joshua, Mr D. Rosser, Mr R. Male, and Mr J. Williams. Several of the songs went well. Dr. Dickson elicited great applause in his rendering of "Old John Barleycorn," the audience all joining in the chorus. The manner in which Mr F. Joshua mastered "The Friar of Orders Grey," is also worthy of commendation, he possessed a fine baritone voice, and knows how to use it to advantage. Mr Male brought the house down in his rendering of the comic song "It makes a man look such a fool." Miss Julia Thomas in her rendering of "Some Day," was deservedly encored by the audience, to which she responded in singing part of the same song again. Mdme S. A. Williams, Mr Tom Morgan, and Mr D. Rosser, as might be expected, did their parts in their usual masterly manner, though Mdme. S. A. Williams seemed to be suffering from the effects of a cold, which considerably affected her voice.—The concert was very fairly attended, considering that the club had not been put to much expense in connection with the undertaking.

———

FUNDRAISING FOR THE RUGBY CLUB
A newspaper report from the "Pontypridd Chronicle" of October 15, 1881.
This is the first recorded fundraising event in aid of the Pontypridd club.

died he had rejoiced in the success of the Welsh XV in Scotland. All available reports were requisitioned to his bedside and read to him by his wife. Tom died on 4th February 1913, aged 53, and was buried at Llethrddu Cemetery, Trealaw.

As the playing career of the young Tom Williams had advanced in the early 1880s, so the fortunes of the Pontypridd club slowly gathered pace. There were, of course, setbacks. The fixture list improved, but matches were postponed and heavy defeats were occasionally suffered. There were player shortages. But there was no lack of determination or ambition.

Pontypridd match reports in the early 1880s were very rare so it is difficult to make conclusions about an overall pattern of success or failure. A disappointment,though, would have been the early cup exit of 1881-82 when the club was unable to repeat the cup run of the previous season. It was reported that Pontypridd had travelled to face Newport in the first round of the South Wales Challenge Cup on 2nd February 1882. This was the first meeting of the two clubs (further evidence of the increasing status of Pontypridd) and Newport won by two goals and three tries to nil. In the 1882 cup final, Newport lost narrowly to Llanelli by a goal to nil.

There were further disappointments in 1882-83 with Pontypridd failing to score in three important matches against Cardiff (twice) and Merthyr. However, they continued to be well-served by the Spickett brothers and Edward Treharne achieved further international recognition by playing against England again on 16th December 1882. The game at St Helen's, Swansea was Wales' first home match but resulted in another defeat by the English. Although thirteen years were to pass before the next Pontypridd representative in the National XV, the club's permanent part in the early days of international rugby had been established :

First international match - Edward Treharne

First international victory - Tom Williams

First home international - Edward Treharne

THOMAS WILLIAMS

Tom Williams was Pontypridd's second 'cap' and first 'winner' in the game against Ireland in 1882. Other success followed throughout his rugby life as an administrator, selector, referee and touch-judge. He 'was there' against the All Blacks in 1905 !

The club's defeats could not detract from a feeling of consolidation by Pontypridd amongst the South Wales clubs. Cardiff were played regularly until 1884. Indeed, the Cardiff club's records show that on 26th December 1883 they lost at home to a Pontypridd side reduced to 14 men when James Spickett left the field. By January 1884 the club was fielding a second XV, a vital development to back up the now regular first team fixtures with the likes of Newport, Merthyr, South Wales University College and Cardiff Harlequins. Another major landmark was the first fixture against the mighty Llanelli on 25th October 1884. The Stradey club played in six of the seven finals of the South Wales Challenge Cup between 1881 and 1887.

Meanwhile, individuals brought further honours to the club. In November 1883, Edward Treharne was selected to play for South Wales against Oxford University. For some reason he never played, but it was reported that Walter Morgan and H.Vivian of Pontypridd did. On 1st December 1883, William Spickett played for Glamorgan against Yorkshire in Cardiff, and then played in an East Wales team against West Wales. This was a final trial before picking the Welsh team to play England in Leeds on 4th January 1884. Spickett was not selected but Edward Treharne was a reserve.

By 1885, unfortunately, there were signs that Pontypridd's period of consolidation was coming to an end. On 7th February a heavy defeat by Newport in the South Wales Challenge Cup was an indication of the hard times around the corner. The years of consolidation were to be followed by the years of struggle.

CLUB MATCHES AFTER 1882

Only one match was reported in 1881-82 - the defeat in the first round of the cup at Newport in February 1882. From December 1882, Pontypridd's fortunes on the pitch were chronicled with more regularity.

1882-1883

23rd December 1882 - CARDIFF v. PONTYPRIDD

"Pontypridd were defeated at Cardiff Arms Park by 1 Goal, 1 Try (disputed) and 3 Touchdowns to 0. The goal was placed by W.Williams from a Try by Simson, while the disputed Try was scored by Hinton."

Cardiff 1 Goal, 1 Try and 3 Touchdowns; Pontypridd 0

11th January 1883 - MERTHYR v. PONTYPRIDD

Team : *Back : Edwards; Threequarters : Arthurs, Watts (Harlequins), and James Spickett; Halves : William Spickett and De Candier; Forwards : R.L.Lewis, Matthews, Lloyd, Thompson, Llewellyn, Harris, J.Daniel, J.W.Jones.*

"One of the best contested matches of the season was played between these clubs at Penydarren Park on this Thursday. In the morning it had rained hard, but fortunately cleared in the afternoon. The ground, however, was very heavy. Pontypridd won the toss, and took the hill. Merthyr kicked off, and for a few minutes play was wild, but afterwards both teams settled down, and played well on the ball; a few long runs were made up to halftime but neither line was much threatened.

On resuming the game, Pontypridd having lost one of their quarterbacks kicked off. They followed up well, and at one time seriously threatened the Merthyr goal; but the hard play of the Merthyr forwards drove the ball back well into the Pontypridd 25. From then until the end of the game Pontypridd were pressed, and F.James got the ball, ran through the Pontypridd pack, but was collared on the goal-line;

he however managed to pass to R.Phillips, who ran in and scored a Try, which S.Thomas turned into a Goal. The ball was again kicked off. The uphill game was too much for the visitors, playing as they were two men short (one of their forwards having to leave twenty minutes after halftime), and after a few scrimmages S.Thomas, getting hold of the ball, made an excellent run, getting in and placing the ball right between the posts, which he turned into a Goal. At the call of time the game stood at……."

Merthyr 2 Goals and 3 Touchdowns; Pontypridd 0

There was further match comment in the "Merthyr Express" :

"Conspicuous for their play in the Pontypridd team were James Spickett, William Spickett (Back), and R.L.Lewis (Forward). Great interest was taken in this match by a large number of spectators, amongst whom we observed a good sprinkling of the Fair Sex".

13th January 1883 - CARDIFF v. PONTYPRIDD

Team : *Back : G.Williams; Threequarters : J.Spickett (captain), D.Treharne; Halves : Arthurs, W.Spickett; Forwards : Rees, R.Lewis, Llewellyn, Morgan, Evans, D.Jenkins, Trevellet, Phillips.*

"In front of a modest crowd at Cardiff Arms Park, Pontypridd were thrashed by 3 Goals, 10 Tries, and 7 Touchdowns to 0."

Cardiff 3 Goals, 10 Tries and 7 Touchdowns; Pontypridd 0

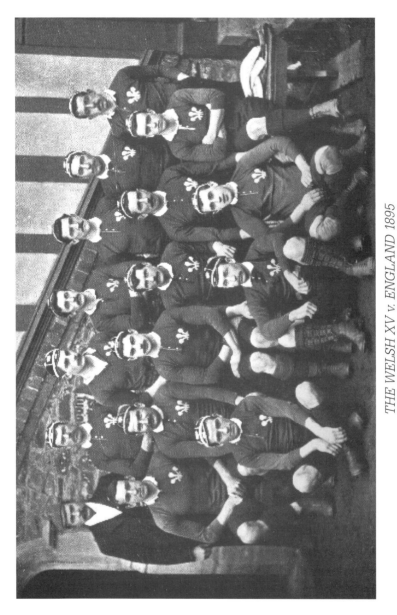

THE WELSH XV v. ENGLAND 1895

Tom Williams the touch-judge (left of back row). A team captained by the immortal Arthur Gould at St Helen's Ground, Swansea.

1883-1884

A RED-LETTER BOXING DAY

26th December 1883 - CARDIFF v. PONTYPRIDD

Team : Back : W.Morris; Threequarters : G.A.Williams, P.M.Arthur, J.Spickett; Halves : W.Spickett (captain), R.J.Cook, M.Rees; Forwards : G.Thomas, Hunt, R.L.Lewis, E.Llewellyn, J.D.Jones, Edward Williams, E.Matthews, J.Davies.

"The weather was decidedly bad and the ground was in a very soft condition, but notwithstanding this, the visiting spectators were very numerous. The Pontypridd men were in exceptionally good form, and seemed more at home on the slippery ground than the home team. Cardiff scored 2 Tries, but failed to convert them. One of the Tries was disputed, the Pontypridd men claiming that Cardiff had 16 men on the field at the time !

James Spickett was injured early in the game and was forced to leave the field. Despite playing with 14 men, Pontypridd fought back, and F.M.Arthur scored 2 Tries for them, one of which was converted by George Williams. The match resulted in a win for the visitors......"

Cardiff 2 Touchdowns and 2 Tries; Pontypridd 1 Goal and 2 Tries

A first victory over Cardiff in the first Boxing Day fixture between the two teams. Indeed a red letter day for the Pontypridd club, its players and its supporters.

10th January 1884 - MERTHYR SECOND XV v. PONTYPRIDD SECOND XV

Team : Back : J.Brown; Threequarters : Roderick, Morris, M.Rees; Halfbacks : A.Coombes (captain), W.Jenkins and T.Jones; Flying man : T.Saunders; Forwards : R.Davies, T.Davies, T.Evans, J.Lewis, T.E.Lewis, Walters, Joe Brooks.

"The ball was kicked off for Merthyr at Penydarren Park by Davies, and from then until the call of time the game was very warmly contested. The Pontypridd men played a good rough game, their forwards being by far the best. Saunders made several runs for them, but he generally lost ground more than he gained..."

Merthyr Second XV 2 Touchdowns; Pontypridd Second XV 1 Touchdown

6th March 1884 - SOUTH WALES UNIVERSITY COLLEGE v. PONTYPRIDD

Team : *Back : T.Jones; Threequarters : T.Williams, Herbert Jones, J.Cook; Halves : M.Rees, D.R.Williams; Forwards : J.D.Jones, E.Llewellyn, T.E.Lewis, J.E.Brooks, A.D.James, E.Roderick, D.Jenkins, E.Rees, D.J.Walters. Umpires : University - Mr G.Elmitt; Pontypridd - Mr Rees.*

"On a Thursday afternoon in pleasant weather, these teams met at Sophia Gardens, Cardiff. The ball was set in motion by L.C.Thomas, the College Captain, and the initial scrimmage was formed inside the Pontypridd 25. The visitors were soon compelled to concede a touchdown, and after the collegians had obliged in a similar manner, W.J.Phillips gained a Try for the homesters. Thomas made capital attempt for goal, but the ball passed just outside the bar. Just before halftime, Thomas got in, but as the legality of the point was questioned, the place kick was not attempted.

The second period rivalled its predecessor in exciting play and well balanced packs; the only points registered were a couple of Minors for the visitors. The forwards were splendidly matched. Thomas Davies, Phillips and Jordan were the most conspicuous of the college backs, whilst Herbert Jones and Tom Williams did best for Pontypridd behind the scrimmage..."

South Wales University College 2 Tries; Pontypridd 0

1884-1885

A BUSY SEASON AND A FIRST MATCH WITH LLANELLI

As the years of consolidation came to an end, several more matches are reported with mixed results, culminating in a potentially demoralising cup defeat against Newport in February. Pontypridd had also played at Rodney Parade in an early season fixture when they took the place of Weston on 18th October, 1884. They had lost that match, too, by 6 Goals and 3 Tries to nil, which was hardly good preparation for their first fixture against Llanelli the following week.

25th October 1884 - LLANELLI v. PONTYPRIDD

The first visit by Pontypridd to the Stradey Grounds was well reported in "The Llanelli and County Guardian" . Not the least interesting aspects of this match report are the importance of establishing a "good reputation" in the Welsh rugby pecking-order, which seemingly Pontypridd did not have at the start of the match, and the quality of the report itself - it is impressively more analytical and opinionated than the reports seen so far from East Wales. The Llanelli club was well served by the coverage given to its matches by the "Guardian".

"Fears had been raised that the game would have been divested of interest because of the supposed superiority of the home team over the other, but these were subsequently found to be unfounded. People judged the visitors in the light of their game against Newport, when they suffered a heavy defeat. However, it was not known that on that occasion Pontypridd played two men short, and had besides had to accept a substitute. To our readers familiar with the game, we need not say what the absence of one man makes, not to speak of two. The play of Pontypridd proved that their strength had been underestimated, and that though they suffered a calamitous defeat, they were not opponents to be despised. On their way down they had picked up J.Clare, an old

EARLY DAYS AT PONTYPRIDD
A Pontypridd team line-up in 1884-85. This is probably the oldest surviving team photograph

valuable Cardiff player (who played alongside Treharne in the Welsh team), who made himself a tower of strength for them. On several occasions alone he averted the invasion of their goal. The Pontypridd forwards were clearly outmatched, but, excepting the frequent falling on the ball in the scrimmage, waged a plucky flight. By the end, though, the visitors were thoroughly disheartened, their defence had gone to pieces, and much to their relief time was called..."

Llanelli 4 Goals and 2 Touchdowns; Pontypridd 1 touch-in-goal

1st November 1884 - CARDIFF v. PONTYPRIDD

Team : *Back : G.Williams; Threequarters : J.Clare, W.Jenkins; Halves : G.Williams and D.Williams; Forwards : R.Lewis, W.Williams, E.Llewellyn, Cook, T.Davies, Lott, Gould, Norman.*

The week following the Llanelli game, Pontypridd travelled to Cardiff Arms Park. The match report stated that the visitors arrived four men short, and in order to make a game of it the home team gave the services of two of their players - Clare (again !) and Norman - and at the same time reduced its own team to 13 men. As it was, Cardiff had it all their own way and won by 8 goals and 4 tries to nil, or 22- nil. The "Evening News" reported this match as Cardiff v. Rhondda, but the Cardiff club records it as Cardiff v. Pontypridd. The players certainly look very much like a Pontypridd side.

Cardiff 8 Goals and 4 Tries; Pontypridd 0

By the New Year of 1885, the Pontypridd and Merthyr clubs had established regular playing contact. It is encouraging to see that in January both clubs tried to put out two XVs to play each other on the same day and that honours were shared in the two matches. A puzzle is that whilst the second team had a full complement of 15 players, the premier side turned up at Merthyr two short. Much the same situation applied to Merthyr in reverse. Resources may well have been stretched too far : by the time of the return First XV fixture later that month the supply of players had dried up even more, with controversial results.

8th January 1885 - MERTHYR v. PONTYPRIDD

"These old rivals met in the presence of a company of spectators. The home team played one and the visitors two men short. Merthyr were very strongly represented, but such could hardly be said of Pontypridd. From first to last the home team had it all their own way, and play for the most part was in the visitors half. The ground was very slippery, and would not permit the home backs play to advantage, or the result would have been still more decisive. Merthyr started the ball, and after fifteen minutes hard play Matthews ran in; but the point was disallowed on the plea of offside. Soon after L.C.Thomas crossed the line and obtained a Try for Merthyr, which he also converted into a goal. Nothing, except the visitors touching down, occured up to halftime.

In the second half, Merthyr now having the advantage of the hill, continued to press their opponents. Thomas now made off, and after a dodgy run passed to E.P. Alexander, who obtained a Try; but the kick failed. George Williams restarted for the visitors, and the forwards following up well compelled Merthyr to touch down. The leather once more being in play W.E.Evans made off, but being pressed passed to Phillips, who again passed to Matthews. The last named crossing the line; Thomas took the kick, and converted into a goal. Knapp obtained the next Try from a loose scrimmage, but this time the kick at goal failed. Soon after the visitors again touched down. Pontypridd followed up the kick-out, D.W.Evans (Substitute) obtaining a Try; but the kick by George Williams failed. Time was now called, the game ending in victory for Merthyr........

Steard, Mog Rees, Milward and D.W.Evans played well for Pontypridd, the excellent play of George Williams at Back, saved their goal-line time after time."

Merthyr 2 Goals, 2 Tries and 2 Touchdowns; Pontypridd 1 Try

8th January 1885 - PONTYPRIDD SECOND XV v. MERTHYR
SECOND XV

Team : Back : A.Lott; Threequarters : Alfred Lewis, T.E.Lewis (captain), John Williams; Halves : G.Gould and Tom Harry; Forwards :

Rees Davies, J.Thomas, J. Lewis, W.Plumpton, T.B.Evans, Ivor Howells, Joe Brooks, W.Lewis, W.Evans.

"This return match between these teams was played at the Ynysangharad field on Thursday, and resulted in a very easy victory for the home team. The tries were obtained by T.E.Lewis, Gould, Thomas, and Tom Harry, and the goals kicked by Lott. In justice to Merthyr it may be stated that they could only muster up nine of their team, but on arriving at Pontypridd they were supplemented by three very good substitutes, thus making their number 12, as against 15 of the home team, who also had not an extra good team, in consequence of some of their number going to Merthyr with the first team in order to make up a team. The match was very friendly and pleasant throughout."

Pontypridd Second XV 2 Goals, 2 Tries, 6 Touchdowns and 1 touch-in-goal; Merthyr Second XV 0

18th January 1885 - MERTHYR v. PONTYPRIDD

"The visitors turned up with only 9 men, while the home team were strongly represented, including two international players, L.C.Thomas and E.Alexander (both Brecon), and one international reserve, A.A.Matthews (Lampeter), and an old international player W.F.Evans (Rhymney). The visitors borrowed 3 men and played 3 men short...."

Merthyr 1 Goal and 2 Tries; Pontypridd 1 Try and 2 Touchdowns

The defeat at Merthyr had not been particularly heavy, and Pontypridd were understandably aggrieved by their opponents liberal use of international "guests". However, the match report in the "Evening News" points again to a shortage of players, or even unreliable players, that was bedevilling the club throughout 1884-85. There had been an embarrassing situation earlier in the season when on 24th November Pontypridd telegrammed Cardiff Harlequins at 2.45 p.m. to say that they would not be fulfilling that afternoon's away fixture as they could not raise a team. Ironically, a match was eventually played against the 'Quins on 16th February. Playing at home, and using several second team men, Pontypridd won by 1 Goal, 2 Tries and 4 Touchdowns to 1 Touchdown and 1 touch-in-goal.

There is one further twist in this sorry tale. Barely three weeks after the defeat of the depleted team to the "All Stars" at Merthyr, Pontypridd played an important cup match at Newport and themselves resorted to guest players to which the Newport captain, in turn, objected.

7th February 1885 - NEWPORT v. PONTYPRIDD
South Wales Challenge Cup - Round 1

Team : Back : George Williams; Threequarters : W.Williams, Norman, Clare; Halves : W.Jenkins, M.Rees, J.Jones; Forwards : R.C.Lewis, D.Davies, J.Davies, G.Thomas, Mrecott, Hinton, E.Lewis, E.Llewellyn.

"Having already suffered some humiliating defeats, Pontypridd's luck was completely out when they were drawn away to Newport... The match was played in the presence of a large number of spectators. The ground was in a dreadful state owing to the heavy rain of the past week, and good play was really out of the question. The Pontypridd team did not arrive until half an hour after the arranged kick-off time and it was at once seen that in physique the home team were far superior, and little doubt was felt as to the ultimate result. The Newport captain at once objected to Clare, Norman and Hinton (Cardiff men) being included in the Pontypridd team. Despite this, the game was started, and Newport began to score Tries at regular intervals. Midway through the second half, Pontypridd had lost all interest, and their tackling was feeble......"

Newport 62; Pontypridd 0 (approximate score)

This was indeed a demoralising defeat. That the Cardiff Reserves then beat the Pontypridd First XV the following Saturday at Cardiff Arms Park, albeit narrowly by 10 points to 3, did not help. Unfortunately, the performance at Newport was a harbinger of further difficulties awaiting the club in the next two or three years.

CHAPTER 4

1885-88 - YEARS OF STRUGGLE

It is difficult to assess the full effect of the terrible cup defeat of February 1885 on the Pontypridd club. It would have been unusual if the fledgling outfit had not borne some mental scars the following September when the new season commenced. Ironically, the fixture list took them to Newport on 26th September 1885 for what in boxing parlance would have been described as a "rematch". Though Pontypridd lost again, reports of a "well contested" performance suggest a reasonable recovery from the trauma of the previous winter. Unfortunately, deeper problems awaited the club in the next three years.

The years of struggle were not without their moments of hope. The fact that Newport retained the Pontypridd fixture and even played their first match in the town in 1886 indicates the club's position, however tenuous, in the South Wales elite. Indeed, yet more new clubs such as Penarth, Mountain Ash and Grangetown were now played and, significantly, the fixtures were further expanded to include the last of the "Big Four", Swansea, in January 1888. These were the years, too, when the personalities continued to light up the dark days of winter. Where previously there had been the Spicketts, Treharnes and Tom Williams, there was now the less celebrated but equally important Eddie Llewellyn and Jack Williams.

There were, perhaps, the first signs of problems ahead. There is some evidence of the departure of influential players. The names of William Spickett, Tom Williams and Edward Treharne appear increasingly in the Cardiff team lists by the mid-1880s, and it was not good for Pontypridd's aspirations that the Cardiff fixture itself was now against "Cardiff Reserves" and was to result in three successive defeats between October 1885 and January 1886.

Pontypridd continued to play in the South Wales Challenge Cup losing in 1886 to Carmarthen at Swansea (when the "Western Mail" reported "The Pontypriddians...played with remarkable stubborness") and to Llanelli the following year (the "Llanelli and County Guardian" lamenting that "No one ever doubted for a moment the issue of the match"). The Cup itself was also in decline. The first-class clubs withdrew from the competition in 1887, to be followed by the remaining Welsh clubs in 1896 whereupon the cup disappeared into bank vaults for over 70 years. Already in its short history rugby in Wales was learning that not only clubs but their competitions and indeed the national union itself would suffer peaks and troughs in their development.

Not even the leaders of the Welsh Football Union were immune to bad days. Whatever their travails on the pitch, the men of Pontypridd continued to be influential off it. At the Annual General Meeting of the Union in the summer of 1886 it was a Pontypridd delegate who asserted that the Union's secretary since its inception, Richard Mullock of Newport, should be replaced by a fresher man, and accordingly proposed Mr Wilkins of Llanelli. In the best traditions of the Welsh Rugby Union of later generations, Mullock had already become a controversial figure, but he survived the subsequent vote and stayed on as secretary for another six years.

One of the more encouraging features for Pontypridd in a difficult period was the establishment of a settled side for most games. A sense of continuity was apparent in the teams listed in the still irregular match reports. A surviving 1886-87 fixture card shows that the headquarters were the Maltsters Arms and that the matches were played on the Trallwng Field and at Ynysangharad Field. The latter was owned by the Newbridge Chainworks' manager, Gordon Lenox. Though still referred to by supporters as "the Red and Blacks" the club colours were in fact Cardinal and Black hoops. Amongst all the regular players now turning out, Pontypridd had its very own John Williams at full-back .

John, or 'Jack' Williams was the stuff of legend. His grandson recalls that as a youngster he was told that Jack used to kick goals

GORDON LENOX

L. Gordon Lenox, JP, was an early benefactor. As well as employing the likes of Jack Williams at Newbridge Chainworks, he gave the club use of Ynysangharad field in the 1880s.

from his own half - thus staking a claim to be the first in a long line of feared Pontypridd goal kickers. Jack lived in Trallwng and worked in the Newbridge Chainworks before dying of pneumonia at the age of 46. The fatal illness was caused, it seems, by Jack calling in to his local pub to quench his thirst after coming directly off his shift at the furnaces.

Another character at this time was John Davies Phillips, who captained the reserve team in 1886-87. In 1881 he was a mere labourer, but married into money and went on to become a successful businessman. A relative of Edgar Phillips, who let the club use the Trallwng Field, he owned several cars and coaches and offered a reliable taxi service around the town; he sometimes carried the team to away fixtures. He was also an undertaker, and later owned the Lamb and Flag in Pentrebach Road. This was opportune (or perhaps not). 'JD' once appeared in court for assaulting the landlord of the New Inn Hotel after a barmaid refused to serve him because he was too drunk. Another contract he held was with the post office to deliver mail from Pontypridd to the Rhondda, boasting two deliveries a day.

With J.E. Brooks owning several hairdressing and tobacco shops in the town, as well as holding a wholesale contract for the whole of the Rhondda valleys, the 'football' club had a strong bearing on the commercial life of the area !

The satisfaction of fielding a regular line-up began to evaporate in 1887-88. The new season saw Pontypridd again trying to field three teams - the First XV, the Reserves and the "A" Team. In so doing they may have been over-ambitious. Match reports were few and far between for the season and in later years it was reported that at this time they were struggling to field a team. Two victories were chronicled, against Grangetown and Penarth, the historic first fixture was played against Swansea, and the now almost customary heavy defeat was endured at the hands of Newport. A season of undoubted struggle was followed by an even worse fate in the dying weeks of 1888.

Following a pre-season nine-a-side tournament at the Cardiff Harlequins ground, Pontypridd played at least three matches before

Christmas. The third of these was a heavy defeat at Bridgend on 15th December and is the final report of the season. Another nine-a-side tournament did take place at Trallwng Field on Christmas Day where the festive spirit was evident. The prize was a bag containing half-a-guinea each to the winning team. A Pontypridd player, William Williams, entered a team called the Pontypridd Lillywhites which contained several Pontypridd players. The final, however, was between Commercial Rovers, of Treforest, and Nixon's Colliery Boys, of Mountain Ash. It is questionable how much of that festive spirit was enjoyed by the local players. There is no further mention of them that day or for the rest of the season. As the old year ended so did, for the time being, the rugby club at Pontypridd.

TWO BIG CUP MATCHES

Although Pontypridd were to make an "early exit" from the South Wales Challenge Cup in both 1886 and 1887, the matches were difficult ones that took them to West Wales in successive years. Significantly, newspaper coverage was becoming far more detailed by this time.

6th February 1886 - CARMARTHEN v. PONTYPRIDD
South Wales Challenge Cup - Round 1 - at Swansea

Team : John Williams; Threequarters : Alf Lewis, W.Jenkins, R.Evans; Halfbacks : Tom Harry and M.W.Rees; Forwards : R.Davies, F.Tilke, R.Rogers, George Gould, Eddie Gould, H.Lewis, J.Thomas and Eddie Llewellyn (captain).
Umpires : Carmarthen - Mr Owen Norton; Pontypridd - Mr J. Gould
Referee : Mr W.Bryant (Secretary, Swansea Football Club)

Reported in the "Carmarthen Journal", 12th February 1886 :

".......Holmes kicked off for Carmarthen about twenty minutes to three. Some loose passing by the latter lost ground, and scrimmages were formed in the centre. Arthurs made off and passed to George Lewis, who skirted the Pontypridd forwards, after which the backs exchanged kicks, the ball eventually left in neutral ground, Arthurs and George Lewis made a good bit of passing and running and invaded the Pontypridd quarters, and the forwards being well up, the goal was put in danger, until A.Lewis ran out. The Pontypridd forwards dribbled and rushed the ball to central ground, but again Arthurs and Lewis carried the ball back to their opponents quarters. Eddie Gould relieved the pressure for Pontypridd and got a few yards outside the 25, where the match was hotly contested, both sides holding their own for some time. Loose and tight scrimmages followed in quick succession in central ground. Arthurs tried to get off, but was thrown by Evans, Smith took the leather near the Pontypridd quarters. The ball was then rushed about six yards from the latter's goal line, but the siege was raised for a few seconds, and then E.W.Davies passed to Arthurs, who cleared his opponents and got a Try in an excellent position which Holme converted into a Goal - the score now reading Carmarthen 18 points, Pontypridd 0.

Shortly after the kick-off, Pontypridd had to defend their quarters against the smart runs of their opponents' backs, but Carmarthen lost much ground by indifferent and wild passing. For 5 minutes some very fast play ensued, play being near the visitors' line. John Williams averted a possible try or touchdown by kicking out just in time, but it was soon returned, and then the Pontypridd forwards rallied and dribbled to central ground. Arthurs kicked along the ground and followed up the same, and by the aid of another kick sent the ball over the goal line, crossed over, picked up, and took his time to ground it down, scoring another Try which Holmes converted into a Goal.

Pontypridd now played up well, and were evidently not discouraged by the rather heavy score placed against them. George Gould showed good play for Pontypridd in the advance, and the ball was sent over and Carmarthen had to touch down. About two minutes after the kick out Pontypridd made a rapid advance, which their opponents failed to check, and George Gould crossed over and obtained a Try which was not converted.

Half-time score : Carmarthen 36 points, Pontypridd 10.

As soon as play was restarted Pontypridd got into the Carmarthen territory, and Spivey dribbled out, but only to be returned. Arthurs came to the rescue, picked up and passed to George Lewis, who got in the open, but Pontypridd would not be denied, and soon got near their opponents' goal line and forced the ball over, Holmes only just being in time to touch down and save the try. After the kick out some loose play ensued in neutral ground, and then Pontypridd once again got into their opponents' 25, Eddie Gould showing some hard play. The homesters now had to play a strictly defensive game for some time and the match was warmly contested. Carmarthen then rushed the ball well up, Arthurs got possession, and made a short and dodgy run which puzzled his opponents; he got over and obtained his third Try, which Holmes failed to convert. The ball was left, after three minutes play, in the home 25. Alf Lewis (Pontypridd) caught the ball from a kick off George Lewis, and the former ran over and obtained a Try, taking his opponents somewhat by surprise. No goal resulted. No other score was recorded."

This almost breathless report certainly creates a sense of movement to and fro. It reads almost like a "ball-by-ball" commentary in modern day cricket ! The "Western Mail" struck a more reflective tone :

"This match...resulted as I anticipated. The Carmarthen men won, but if it had not been for the help of the splendid threequarter, Arthurs, I must confess I should probably have found myself a poor prophet. The Pontypriddians, indeed, played with remarkable stubborness, and if it had not been for the successful place kicking of Holmes, the score would only have been 28-20, instead of 48-20 to Carmarthen."

Carmarthen 48 points; Pontypridd 20.

3rd March 1887 - LLANELLI v. PONTYPRIDD
South Wales Challenge Cup - Round 1

Team : *J.Williams; Threequarters : G.Gould, B.Tiley, W.Phillips, T.Harry; Halves : D.H.Lewis and W.Jenkins; Forwards : W.Williams (captain), E.Llewellyn, J.Mathias, E.Gould, T.Rogers, F.Tilke, A.Lott.*

The "Llanelli and County Guardian" reported that the cup tie was played at the Stradey Grounds in lovely weather. The kick-off was at 3.30 p.m., and the admission charge 6d. The decisive defeat was not without some consolation for the Pontypridd club.

"If a stranger had witnessed the match, he would have come to the conclusion that the Llanelli team had arranged a fixture for the sole purpose of getting practice in the passing game. All the elements which usually attach to a cup fixture were absent : there was no excitement, no rough play, no disputes, and very few exhibitions of really meritorious play. There was a fairly large "Field", which, after the first few minutes play, treated the game with almost entire nonchalance. The Llanelli team were composed of the men that met Cardiff on the previous Saturday, but their form was infinitely inferior to that which they showed against the Cardiffians. Their indifferent play was due, undoubtedly, to the fact that the issue was foregone, and a dislike to "rub it in" to an inordinate extent. The Pontypriddians played a plucky little game towards the close, and put in some excellent play. For the first quarter of an hour, however, there was no attempt at defence at all; but after sides had been changed the visitors warmed to their work, and showed skill in the collaring department, which would have done credit to a more famous team. The match above all things was friendly - this indeed was the distinguishing feature - and in this respect it presented a striking contrast to other games. There were no special incidents in the game. For Pontypridd Ben Tiley did far and away the greatest amount of work, and was invaluable to his team.

Howells kicked off down the gradient, and Pontypridd failing to return, a scrum ensued in the visitors' 25. Bowen was given possession from the scrum and essayed the "Trick", but the ball went wide, and a touchdown only resulted. Tiley set the ball rolling, and G.Griffiths replied. Powell after receiving the leather from Bowen added another Minor to the score. The 25 of the visitors again became the venue of the game, and Bowen getting the ball from a scrimmage dropped a pretty good goal. Howells strove to emulate his captain's performance, but the ball went wide, but Evan Roberts by a smart run secured the leather and scored a Try amid loud cheers. Bowen converted.....

Shortly after the restart, the Llanelli captain crossed the line, and another goal resulted . Williams dribbled the ball in lieu of kicking off, but Llanelli retorted with some good play, and a Touchdown, followed by a converted Goal, were quickly added to the score. "Gitto" got the next Try, but the attempt at goal was not successful.

In the second half, the visitors played up pluckily and frequently showed some pretty play, but it was "no go", and they had to leave the arena with the score......

No one ever doubted for a moment the issue of the match. It was known from the beginning that Pontypridd would not stand a chance against one of the cup holders. Subsequent events confirmed these anticipations. Pontypridd made no show at all, and the home fellows did as they liked with them. It would be a blessed boon if every defeated team took the "Agony" with such grace as Pontypridd."

Llanelli 4 Goals, 3 Tries and 7 Minors; Pontypridd 0.

TWO 'FIRSTS' WITH NEWPORT AND SWANSEA

Though consistent success on the playing field proved elusive, Pontypridd continued to improve the fixture list. In October 1886, they would have been delighted to have a home game with a major club such as Newport and also to be able to field a fairly settled team. Even then, though, the captain, G.Lewis, played as a forward just a week after playing in the threequarters in a club match at Cardiff Harlequins. This, of course, was a not uncommon practice at the time. Equally satisfying 15 months later was being able to play Swansea for the very first time, home or away.

9th October 1886 - PONTYPRIDD v. NEWPORT

Team : J.Williams; Threequarters : W.Williams, T.Harry, A.Lewis; Halves : W.Jenkins, D.Chilcott; Forwards : G.Lewis (captain), E.Llewellyn, Rogers, Tilke, A.Lott, G.Gould, E.Gould, I.Edwards, D.Davies.

"...Played in the presence of a good number of spectators, the game resulted in a victory for the Newport team by 6 Tries to 0. Shortly after the commencement of the game, Pontypridd were deprived of the services of one of their best men, through Alf Lewis being disabled, and another of their threequarters was unable to play, he having twisted a knee at a practice game. Tries were obtained for Newport by Thomas, Powell, and Peveral. George Gould and D.Davies were probably the best for the home team, the latter dribbling and running splendidly. The Pontypridd Volunteer band played a selection of music during the progress of the match."

Pontypridd 0; Newport 6 Tries

7th January 1888 - SWANSEA v. PONTYPRIDD

Team : Back : John Williams; Threequarters : Tom Harry, William Williams (captain), A.N.Other; Halves : George Gould and D.Gimlette;

Forwards : G.Macpherson, Robert Cummings, F.Tilke, D.Davies, Eddie Gould, Tom Nicholas, E.Morgan, H.Lewis, I.Richards.

"......The atmospheric conditions were most unpleasant. Several of the Swansea men, however, were engaged in the international trial match at Cardiff. W.H.Jones got a first half converted Try for Swansea, but the visitors retaliated with an unconverted Try. D.Gwyn got another Try for the homesters just before halftime, and at lemon time the score stood at Swansea 1 Goal and 1 Try, Pontypridd 1 Try.

In the second half the game was entirely in favour of the home side. W.H.Jones made a splendid run from halfway to score his second Try, beneath the posts, then Reid secured yet another Swansea Try."

Swansea 3 Goals, 2 Tries and 4 Minors; Pontypridd 2 Tries.

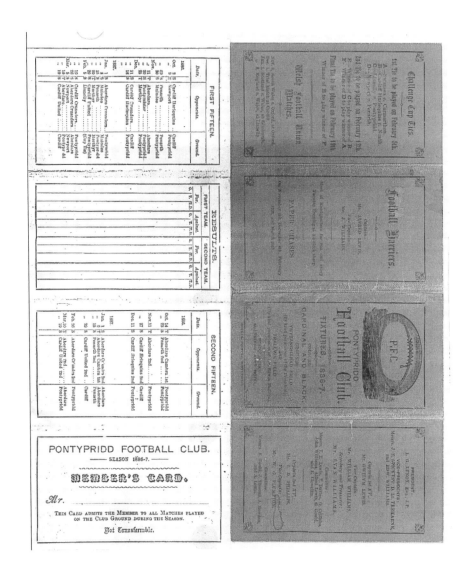

FIXTURE LIST FOR 1886-87
In this season, Gordon Lenox was the Club President and James Spickett a Vice President. The fixtures list both First and Second XV games. The club captain was Gwilym Lewis with home games shared between Ynysangharad and Trallwng fields.

OTHER CLUB MATCHES - 1885-1888

No fewer than 25 other matches were reported in some form or other in the period between September 1885 and Christmas of 1888. They show a number of new opponents on the fixture list and with mixed results.

26th September 1885 - NEWPORT v. PONTYPRIDD

"A fairly well contested match was played between these teams in the presence of around 1,000 spectators. The visitors won the toss, and Clapp kicked off for the home team from the Nursery End. In a short while Pontypridd had to touch down in self defence, but the visitors shortly afterwards drove up the ground in very good form, and the same fate befell Newport. A good deal of even but rough play ensued with varying advantage, until at length Newport worked down, and F.C.Jones (Halfback) obtained possession, passed to Clapp along the line. The Captain, unable to get in, sent the ball to Hannen, who landed a Try between the posts, from which R.Gould kicked a neat conversion for Newport.

After the kick-off from mid-district, Pontypridd drove away to their opponents' line. Their efforts to get over, however, were frustrated by the good combination on the part of the Newport team, who eventually got the ground clear, and Jordan, to whom the ball was sent, obtained the second Try. Gould failed his attempt to 'place' it.

Pontypridd again well followed up the re-start of the ball, and got up to the Newport 25, but after a tight struggle the game was again reversed, and Clapp got a third Try for the home players, but no goal resulted. The remainder of the game, though well contested at every stage by Pontypridd, went all in favour of Newport. R.Gould got over the line and claimed a Try, from which he kicked a goal under protest. Jordan, receiving the ball from F.C.Jones, landed another between the posts, but the kick struck the bar. Once again Jordan got over, and this time Gould kicked the goal."

Newport 3 Goals, 3 Tries and 1 Touchdown; Pontypridd 1 Try

3rd October 1885 - PONTYPRIDD v. CARDIFF RESERVES

This was the first of three games played against the Cardiff second team after the latter had decreed that the First XV was too strong for Pontypridd.

Pontypridd 5; Cardiff 7

24th October 1885 - MOUNTAIN ASH v. PONTYPRIDD

"A match between these sides was played on Saturday. For the home team J.Williams, Ben Tiley, and J.Carey played splendidly. The try scored for Mountain Ash was gained by Ben Tiley..."

Mountain Ash 1Try and 1 Touchdown; Pontypridd 1 Try (disputed) and 1 Touchdown

5th December 1885 - CARDIFF RESERVES v. PONTYPRIDD

Team : *G.Williams; Threequarters : A.Lewis, W.Williams, M.W.Rees; Halves : J. Randall and W.Davies; Forwards : D.Davies, T.Davies, J.Yorath, J.Williams, R.Lewis, J.Thomas, H.Gould, T.Rogers, F.Tilke.*

"The return match at Cardiff Arms Park was played in an incessant downpour of rain, the ground was therefore in a slippery condition, and the number of good runs was limited. The ball was kicked off at 3.15 by Pontypridd from the Westgate Street end. A few minutes later the ball was rushed over the visitors' goal-line, and compelled them to touch down in defence. On the kick out, Norton got possession, but was collared before he got too far. The Pontypridd forwards then made a rush and carried the ball over the Cardiff goal-line, and compelled them to touch down. The ball was then taken down to the Pontypridd 25, and W.Evans, getting possession of it, ran and scored a Try, but it was not converted. The play for some minutes afterwards was in neutral territory, but the oval was eventually dribbled into the visitors 25, when Norton made a good run, but failed to get over the line. From a scrimmage, Thomas scored another home Try, the kick again failing. Almost from the kick out, Morgan secured another Try, but the major points were not added.

After half-time, James rushed in for another Cardiff Try, the place kick being successful. The other score of the half was a Try by A.Lewis for the visitors."

Cardiff Reserves 1 Goal, 3 Tries & 2 Touchdowns; Pontypridd 1 Try & 1 Touchdown

2nd January 1886 - CARDIFF RESERVES v. PONTYPRIDD

This third defeat in as many months for Pontypridd at the hands of the Cardiff seconds was not reported.

Cardiff Reserves 15; Pontypridd 0.

14th February 1886 - PONTYPRIDD v. CARDIFF HARLEQUINS

This was the last match recorded in 1885-86 and resulted in a much needed victory for Pontypridd.

Pontypridd 1 Goal, 2 Tries & 1 Touchdown; Cardiff Harlequins 1 Touchdown & 1 Touch-in-goal

2nd October 1886 - CARDIFF HARLEQUINS v. PONTYPRIDD

Team : *G.Williams; Threequarters : G.Lewis (Captain), J.Davies, A.Lewis, T.Harry; Halves : W.Jenkins, D.Chilcott; Forwards : E.Llewellyn, W.Williams, E.Gould, G.Gould, Tilke, A.Lott, I.Edwards, J.Thomas.*

Pontypridd's first game of the new season took them to Cathays in Cardiff. The "Western Mail" reported the new scoring system :

"..The new football rules are as follows - A match shall be decided by a majority of points - a Goal shall equal 3 points, a Try 1 point. If the number of points are equal, or no goal being obtained, the match shall be declared a draw. When a goal is kicked from a Try, the Goal only is scored."

Match Drawn

23rd October 1886 - PENARTH v. PONTYPRIDD

Team : *Williams; Threequarters : Tiley, Matthews, G.Gould, T.Jones; Halves : W.Jenkins, Chilcott; Forwards : W.Williams, Mathias, E.Llewellyn, Rogers, Lott, E.Gould, Idris James, Mercott.*

"The home captain won the toss, and played with a strong wind in his team's favour. The homesters scored a Try and a Touchdown during the early part of the game, before the visitors warmed to the game, and eventually won by 1 Goal, 2 converted Tries (obtained by W.Williams and Ben Tiley) and 6 Minors, to 1 Try and 1 Minor."

A curious fact about this game was that Pontypridd had to fall back on reserves because four of the regulars failed to turn up - G.R.Evans, D.Lewis, D.Davies, and Tilke failing to arrive at the railway station. This must have been a strange experience for Pontypridd, because they rarely travelled with a full side, let alone have four reserves available.

Penarth 1 Try and 1 Minor; Pontypridd 1 Goal, 2 Converted Tries and 6 Minors

On the same day, Pontypridd Reserves defeated Penarth Seconds 10-0 at Taff Vale Park. The Pontypridd Reserves XV was recorded as follows:

S.Nicholas; Threequarters : W.Wilkins, D.Gimlette, T.E.Jones, T.Harry; Halves : J.Thomas, S.Johnson; Forwards : J.D.Phillips (Captain), J.Bowden, W.G.Plumpton, D.Davies, T.Nicholas, Madoc Evans, T.Ayliffe, A.Hughes.

30th October 1886 - PONTYPRIDD v. MAINDEE

Team : *J.Williams; Threequarters : Gimlette, Harry, Tiley, Jones; Halves : Chilcott and Jenkins; Forwards : W.Williams, Mathias, Rogers, Tilke, Edwards, Gould, Lott, Davies.*

"After a well contested game, the home team were declared winners....Tom Harry obtained a fine Try... passing man after man before planting the ball right behind the 'sticks'. For the winners,

Williams (Back), Ben Tiley and Tom Harry (Threequarters), Chilcott and Jenkins (Halfbacks), and Mathias, Williams, Rogers and Tilke (Forwards), all played well."

Pontypridd 1 Try and 2 Minors; Maindee 0

4th November 1886 - PONTYPRIDD 'A' v. OLD BOYS

Team : S.Nicholas; Threequarters : T.Harry, Albert Matthews, T.J.Blobbs, W. Gimlette; Halves : J.Evans, Hogarths and D.Chilcott; Forwards :W.Williams, F.Tilke, Ivor Edwards, Eddie Gould, D.Davies, J.Thomas, Idris James, Abrahamson.

Old Boys (or 'Pals') *: D.T.Lloyd; Threequarters : M.W.Rees, Walter Phillips, J.W. Richards, G.Treharne; Halves : W.T.Davies, Cooke; Forwards : B.Phillips, T.Foster, G.Ward, T.Lewis, R.Rowlands, D.H.Lewis, J.Treharne, and others.*

Pontypridd seemed to have 16 players and their opponents even more ! The Old Boys were made up of ex-Pontypridd players from the Rhondda Valley and some up and coming youngsters. The 'Treharne' in the threequarters may well have been Gwilym, the younger brother of Edward. Tries were scored by Chilcott, W.Williams, Gimlette and Harry, and a Goal was kicked by Nicholas.

Pontypridd 1 Goal and 3 Tries; Old Boys 0

25th November 1886 - PONTYPRIDD v. MERTHYR

Pontypridd won this unreported game by 3 points to 1.

4th December 1886 - NEWPORT v. PONTYPRIDD

Team *: J.Williams; Threequarters : T.Harry, G.Gould, D.Gimlette; Halves : Chilcott and W.Jenkins; Forwards : W.Williams (Captain), Tilke, Mathias, J.D.Phillips, Eddie Gould, Eddie Llewellyn, D.Davies, Locke, Ivor Edwards.*

This match took place just two months after Newport's first visit to Pontypridd.

JOHN DAVIES PHILLIPS

A labourer and captain of the reserve team in 1886-87 who 'made good '.
Based at Lamb and Flag Mews, Pontypridd, Trealow Mews, Trealow,
and the Garage, Merthyr Road, Pontypridd, J.D.Phillips (Cab Proprietor,
Mail Contractor and Funeral Furnisher) *was a flourishing businessman*
in later life.

[Photograph courtesy Wayne Morgan]

"A return fixture between these two sides was arranged at the last moment, and was brought off in the presence of a comparatively small number of spectators. The ground after the frost and a mucky thaw militating against good play. At 3.30, Pontypridd kicked off towards the Nursery End, and Webb made a good return. The visitors failed to send it back with anything like smartness, and Newport at once rushed their line. Williams, the Pontypridd back, however, kicked into touch at the 25 flag, and a series of loose scrums ensued near that spot. Neither side showed any advantage for a little while, with the exception of the fact that the visitors gradually worked to the centre. Without much delay, Newport's C.Thomas got off, and passing to Powell, who transferred to F.C.Jones, who got close to the line but failed to score, and a hard scrimmage ensued outside the visitors' goal. Pontypridd gallantly warded off the attack for several minutes, withstanding determined efforts of the home men to cross the line.

When ends were changed, Newport had all the advantage, penning their opponents in their own half the whole time. Tries were obtained for Newport through Thomas (2), Pepperall, Harding, and Powell, and at the call of 'No-side' the match which was entirely one-sided left the home side winners...."

Newport 1 Goal and 5 Tries; Pontypridd 0

Two very unusual incidents happened in the next two games.

11th December 1886 - CARDIFF CRUSADERS v. PONTYPRIDD

Team : *J.Williams; Threequarters : Ben Tiley, E.Harris, George Gould, W.Jenkins; Halves : D.Chilcott, G.Lewis; Forwards : W.Williams (Captain), Eddie Llewellyn, T.Tilke, Eddie Gould, J.Edwards, Mathias, A.N.Other.*

A week after the Newport game, Pontypridd played the Crusaders at Sophia Gardens. The ground was in a very bad condition, and the game did not run its full course. The Pontypridd team, apparently unhappy with the weather and disputing the referee's decisions on several occasions, walked off ! The home side were leading at the time by 3 Tries and 7 Minors to nil.

Match Unfinished

18th December 1886 - PONTYPRIDD v. CARDIFF HARLEQUINS

Team : *J.Williams; Threequarters : Ben Tiley, Tom Harry, W.Jenkins; Halves : Chilcott and G.Lewis (Captain); Forwards : W.Williams, E.Llewellyn, R.A.Lewis, D.Lewis, T.Mathias, Ivor Edwards, George Gould, J.Bowen, E.Gould.* **Referee :** *Mr D.A.Jones (Oxford University)*

"Both teams were well represented. After playing for about 5 minutes, a serious accident took place. James, the Harlequins' fast man, got hold of the leather, and bolted away in fine style, when Ben Tiley, seeing the danger, sprinted across the field, and the two players met very roughly. James received a nasty blow on the temple, and was carried from the field to the Maltsters' Arms Hotel, where he was attended to by Mr. Davies, assistant to Dr. Hunter. After the accident, the Harlequins' captain, Ferguson, objected to the match being continued, although his men were anxious to proceed without James. Ferguson, however, was very determined, and refused to let his men play, thus terminating the match, that had been looked forward to with a great deal of interest."

Match Terminated

15th January 1887 - PONTYPRIDD v. PENARTH

This unreported game ended in a draw. On Christmas Day, Pontypridd Seconds had played Treforest on the Trallwng Field before "a numerous assemblage of spectators". After a "sharp game" the home side emerged victors.

Match Drawn

29th January 1887 - MERTHYR v. PONTYPRIDD

"The visitors brought up an exceedingly strong team, and were too good for the home men in every way, their passing and following up being splendid. Tiley especially distinguished himself, getting two of the Tries and kicking the Goal from an exceedingly difficult angle."

Merthyr 0; Pontypridd 1 Goal, 3 Tries and 2 Minors

5th March 1887 - NEWPORT v. PONTYPRIDD

Team : *Williams; Threequarters : B.Tiley, W.Phillips, W.Williams (Captain); Halves : G.Gimlette and Thomas; Forwards : E.Llewellyn, Morgan, D.H.Lewis, T.Rogers, E.Gould, Edwards, J.Mathias, Davies, F.Tilke.*

"This was played on a fine, but bitterly cold day, and in the presence of a meagre crowd. Newport held the upper hand throughout the match..."

Newport 2 Goals, 1 Try, and several Minors; Pontypridd 0

This was the last game reported in the 1886-87 season. Although Newport were the only big club to give Pontypridd a regular fixture, it had been a season of some consolidation.

8th September 1887 - PONTYPRIDD v. CARDIFF HARLEQUINS

Pontypridd opened the new season with a match at their now permanent base, Ynysangharad Park. The match report in the "Western Mail" seems to suggest that the sides played for two hours !

"The field was in an unfavourable condition owing to the previous showers of rain. Play commenced at 4.30, and was determined and spirited throughout. The match was continued until 6.30, when dusk impaired, and the inevitable decision was that the game must be a draw in the favour of the Harlequins, who had scored 1 Goal and 1 Minor, to 1 Goal. There was a large number of spectators on the ground."

Pontypridd 1 Goal; Cardiff Harlequins 1 Goal and 1 Minor

15th September 1887 - PONTYPRIDD v. GRANGETOWN

"...Pontypridd faced Grangetown in fine weather, and the ground in good condition. Some capital play was shown on both sides, but neither team secured a goal, but at fulltime Pontypridd were victors..."

Pontypridd 2 Tries; Grangetown 0

Even at this early stage of the new season, it was felt that Pontypridd had not shown much form. The players were advised to "resort to more practice or the well-earned reputation of previous seasons will wane". This was good advice with another match with mighty Newport imminent.

5th November 1887 - NEWPORT v. PONTYPRIDD

Team *: J.Williams; Threequarters : W.Williams (Captain), Ben Tiley, Tom Harry, R. Cummings; Halves : Gould and Gimlette; Forwards : F.Tilke, D.Davies, E.Gould, T.Rogers, D.Jones, R.Jones, I.Edwards, J.Thomas.*

"A comparatively small gate mustered to witness a trial of strength between these clubs. The home team, who had introduced a few new men at forward, kicked off at 3.25 from the Nursery End, and immediately rushed the leather into the Pontypridd half, securing within three minutes a Minor. After the kickout from the 25, Morgan took up and executed another touchdown. The visitors then made an assault on the Newport ground, but the advantage was short lived. Newport drove away to the visitors' end with a rush, and although Pontypridd for a time defended vigorously, Morgan followed up a forward assault and mauled one of the visitors on his line, bringing off another Minor.

The game at this fairly early stage gave promise of a very unequal encounter. After only a few minutes further play, Morgan, from a pass by Harding, got over and secured Newport's first Try, the same player missing the place kick. The re-start from the Pontypridd 25 was a 'Messer', giving Newport a chance of rushing again to the 25. From a scrum, Downe passed to Webb, who put in a decent sprint, and then chucked to F.C.Jones, who galloped over for an easy Try. Although, however, the ball was landed behind the posts, Morgan failed to place the major point. After a brief sojourn at the centre of the field, the 'Mustard and Black' lot scored another Try by E.Jones, which Webb goaled. Following this, the visitors attacked the Newport line and the home side had to wake up to defend.

At the start of the second half the Pontypridd kick off was a failure, and Newport at once advanced, Griffiths taking a pass from Downe, ran in, and Webb kicked the goal but the point was disputed, and the home captain giving way the ball was taken to the centre and a scrum was formed. The visitors spent the rest of the game defending, and only once broke away when they secured a Minor."

Newport 4 Goals, 3 Tries and 6 Minors; Pontypridd 1 Minor

10th November 1887 - MERTHYR v. PONTYPRIDD

"This match was announced to be played at Penydarren Park on Thursday, but owing to the latter team not turning up the match did not take place. No telegram was received, and the home team waited (in the hope that they would come up by brake) from 2.30 until 4 o'clock. It may be stated that arrangements are being made to bring the two teams together, and it is hoped that next time there will be no grounds for complaint given."

24th December 1887 - PENARTH v. PONTYPRIDD

Team : John Williams; Threequarters : Tom Harry, Francis Miles, William Williams (Captain), George Gould; Halves : White and Gimlette; Forwards : J.Edwards, Eddie Gould, E.Morgan, E.James, G.Lewis, Tom Nicholas, Robert Cummings, A.Hughes.

At this time of year, Pontypridd traditionally had difficulty fielding a team. However, the game against Penarth was described as a pleasant one.

Penarth 1 Try and 1 Minor; Pontypridd 0

17th March 1888 - PONTYPRIDD v. PENARTH

Team : John Williams; Threequarters : Ben Tiley, William Williams (Captain), George Gould, Francis Miles; Halves : Thomas and Gimlette; Forwards : Ack Llewellyn, Tom Harry, I.Edwards, Tom Nicholas, Eddie Gould, H.Lewis, E.Morgan, Ivan Edwards.

The return fixture with the seasiders was the last of the few games reported that season. Ben Tiley was in brilliant form and gained a Try for his team by running from his own 25 and then kicked the goal from a difficult angle and into a strong wind.

Pontypridd 1 Goal and 3 Tries; Penarth 0

The victory over Penarth was a pleasing end to a difficult season that had seen the club struggle.

The ill-fated autumn fixtures of 1888 began with a pre-season 9-a-side tournament at the Cardiff Harlequins' ground. Competing teams consisted of 10 men, including a reserve. The field was 66 x 45 yards and the scoring was as follows : Drop Goal 8 points, Try 6 points, Conversions 4 points. The competition was played under handicap rules. Pontypridd's handicap was 10 points, while their first round opponents, Ely Boys, were handicapped at 24 points.

22nd September 1888 - CARDIFF HARLEQUINS' TOURNAMENT

Team : W.Williams (Captain), G.R.Evans, D.H.Lewis, J.Williams, George Gould, D.Gimlette, W.Jenkins, Ben Tiley, and Tom Harry.

"The weather was fine and over 1,000 spectators assembled. In the first round match of 10 minutes each way against Ely Boys it proved an interesting game, and was tight throughout. The teams were equally matched in weight and height but Ely managed to rush the ball over their opponents' line, a touchdown resulting. Pontypridd then became alive to the fact that they must exert themselves, and almost immediately they obtained a Try, which was well converted. Ely returned the compliment, gaining a Try, but the kick at goal was futile. Ely pressed their opponents considerably in the second half and were eventually declared the winners by 32 points to 25."

24th November 1888 - PONTYPRIDD v. LLANDAFF

Team : *John Williams; Threequarters : Tom Harry, George Gould, D.Gimlette, Francis Miles; Halves : James Thomas and William Jenkins; Forwards : William Williams (Captain), Ivor Howells, David Evans, Eddie Llewellyn, Ack Llewellyn, Eddie Gould, S.Nicholas.*

This match was played at Trallwng Field with Pontypridd one man short, and their opponents two. A drawn game ended in Llandaff's favour.

Pontypridd 0; Llandaff 1 Minor point

1st December 1888 - PENARTH v. PONTYPRIDD

The day was cold and dull and the pitch was "little better than a slough".

"...A fair number of spectators were present but the game was mostly confined to the forwards. It was played under new rules and both teams were strange to the alterations. Throughout the game there was a continual blowing of the referee's whistle and cries of 'Free kick !' from the players which caused much amusement..."

Penarth 5 Tries; Pontypridd 1

On 15th December, Pontypridd played their 'final' game at Bridgend and lost by 2 Tries and 9 Minors to nil............

CHAPTER 5

A TEMPORARY DEATH

AFTER December 1888 the Pontypridd club no longer existed. In tracing and celebrating the establishment and determined consolidation of such a town club in the early days of rugby in South Wales, it is perhaps only human to underestimate the setbacks and enduring problems that confronted James Spickett and those who came after him. Perhaps, too, Pontypridd's demise that Christmas was inevitable.

An interesting witness was Eddie Llewellyn. He was first reported as playing for the club in December 1883 in the historic first victory over Cardiff. He became an 'ever-present' at a time when there were recurring problems over fielding a full team. As the Spicketts' professional careers slowly brought an end to their playing days and restricted their involvement with the club, it was people such as Llewellyn who filled the gap they left. He was the club captain in 1885-86.

On 7th May 1891, Eddie Llewellyn gave his explanation as to why the club had collapsed by the end of 1888 :

" *The Pontypridd club, though known as a junior one, is one of the oldest clubs in Wales, and some 10 years ago could boast a team that could make a good fight with any in the Principality. I remember on one occasion we beat Cardiff on their own ground. At that time there were no other clubs in the district, and we had the whole of the Rhondda to pick from. Often we struggled to raise a team. As an instance of this I remember that the season after we beat Cardiff we were to play Cwmbran in the cup and only half our team turned up. As a result we were obliged to scrape up substitutes from Cardiff, and even Cwmbran itself was called upon to make up our team. Efforts were made year after year to organise a team, but all to no avail. Although there were plenty of good players in the district there was the drawback of men being unable to keep together. It was often the case that about Christmas time the interest in football waned, and most of the fixtures were cancelled. Matters went from bad to worse until the season before last, when everybody who had anything to do with the club gave the matter up in despair, thoroughly sick of the whole affair. It was often galling to me to read reports of other teams, knowing full well that Pontypridd, if they only put their shoulder to the wheel, could have held with the best of them."*

Llewellyn's version may be a mix of the realistic and the over-critical. He rightly praises the first victory over Cardiff and identifies a local area that could be a rugby nursery. Yet a picture emerges of an ever-increasing struggle to raise a team, of an embarrassing borrowing of players from other clubs, and, rather dispiritingly even in those far off days, men succumbing to the counter attractions of Christmas. His evocative observation about their need to "put their shoulder to the wheel" complements the fact that there were indeed players to choose from in the Pontypridd area.

At the very time that the Pontypridd club was folding, other outfits were being established in the locality. In that same fateful Christmas of 1888, the Maritime Colliery team were into their second season, had an improving fixture list, and had started to make a name for themselves. They appear to have taken Pontypridd's place in the Cardiff Harlequins' nine-a side competition at the start of the 1889-90 season. The Maritime squad that day included many names who would re-emerge in the future Pontypridd club : B.Dickenson, Harry Williams, J.Merry, S.Sullivan, Harry Stead, G.Thomas, J.Evans, J.Connelly, J.Edwards, and Griffiths.

Whatever the temporary fate of their club, several former Pontypridd players now looked for a game elsewhere. Several joined Treforest or other junior clubs in the town. On 14th December 1889, Treforest played a Cardiff 'A' team at Taff Vale Park and fielded a XV that contained familiar names from the Maritime and former Pontypridd teams. The Treforest line-up was :

Back : J.Owen (captain); Threequarters : W.Morgan, T.Gould, S.Sullivan, J.Miles; Halves : C.Jones, J.Holloway; Forwards : J.Nicholas, D.Thorne, Ack Llewellyn, R.Lane, G.Jones, Thomas Jones, James Edwards, E.W.Thomas.

The name of Ack Llewellyn is an interesting one. He was yet another player, referee and administrator in the Tom Williams' tradition. Clearly a player at the time of Pontypridd's demise, he was refereeing Barbarians' matches in Wales in the late 1890s and, emulating Tom Williams' achievement two years earlier, refereed the England v. Ireland match of 1906. Like Williams he was a Mid-District representative on the Welsh Football Union and features in the great 1905 international against New Zealand - he was the Welsh touch judge. A final claim to fame by Llewellyn, ringing familiar bells in a modern ear, was that in that same year of 1905 he orchestrated a committee of the WFU considering the need for a National Ground. The pace of change in Welsh rugby is sometimes slow !

As a final postscript on the untimely events at the end of 1888 in Pontypridd, Ack Llewellyn wrote an article for the Rhondda Leader on 3rd September 1920. In it he confirmed that he had first played for Pontypridd against Newport in 1888 on the Trallwng Field where the Central Hotel was later built. More significantly, perhaps, Llewellyn goes on to tell us that because of the later loss of its ground the club collapsed.

Between them, Eddie Llewellyn and Ack Llewellyn have probably completed the jigsaw of why the Pontypridd club went out of existence at the end of 1888 : shortage of - and perhaps unreliable - players, poor results, and the loss of a ground together proved an unsurmountable set of disadvantages for a young club at the time. Even then, though, there remained players that believed there should be a town club. Within a short while they began making plans to reform a club that was dead but not buried.

The legacy of the Spicketts' and the Treharnes', the Tom Williams' and Ack Llewellyns', and many other less celebrated names both on and

ACK LLEWELLYN
A distinguished man of Pontypridd who ran the line on the greatest day
of all, December 16th 1905 : Wales 3, New Zealand nil.

off the field, would not be forgotten overnight. The spirit of the club, as epitomised by men like John Daniel Jones, lived on.

Jones had probably been a founder member of the club, and is more than likely the 'Jones' that appears in the earliest match reports. A 'J.D.Jones' was certainly playing regularly in 1880-81. John was born at Bridge Street, Pontypridd in 1861, the son of a draper. He appears to have retired from playing in the summer of 1884, but continued as a committeeman for at least another ten years. In the seasons 1893-94 and 1894-95 he was the club treasurer. When he inherited the family shop in Bridge Street, he supplied the club for several years with its drapery requirements. He was obviously a successful businessman as he later opened the Top Shop in Cilfynydd. John died in a nursing home in Cardiff on 1st February 1924.

There was also the legacy of what might be called a way of sporting life that could not be wiped out and was bound to re-emerge. Significant numbers of young men who were in the habit of playing 'football' at least once, if not twice, a week would still need their recreation. The first Pontypridd players were aged 16 or 17, and today would be regarded as a schoolboys or youth team. They were rarely six feet tall, hardly surprising when the international forwards of 1876 were on average 5 feet 10 inches tall and weighed around 11 stone. Of course, as the club got older so did the players, until they retired and were replaced by the next generation of youngsters.

James Spickett wrote that the players' training consisted chiefly of long walks and sprints to Aberdare, Cardiff, Merthyr, Ferndale, Treherbert and other places for about two months before the season started. Once the season was underway and the club was sometimes playing two matches a week, the players thought that the games themselves were training enough.

The game of rugby has always been associated with a sense of fellowship, but it is difficult to assess how much camaraderie there was off the field at the time. Whilst playing, the 'team' was distinguishable by its Cardinal and Black hoops with long 'shorts' and socks and boots and the captain wore a cap. As in modern times, designs and colours may have changed. An 1884-85 photograph shows the hoops barely visible and probably looked more like a black jersey. Kit may have been supplied by the club through subscriptions from its members. It is also possible that in later years they would go around the shops in the town centre asking for contributions. There was already a sports' shop in the town, but with the sons of drapers playing in the team they probably got the jerseys and shorts at a discounted price.

We know that the club was founded by James Spickett and others at the Butchers Arms and we must assume that this hotel became the first headquarters. But with the club playing at the far north end of the town, the Maltsters' Arms soon became its home. This was far more practical as there were no changing rooms at either Trallwng Field or Ynysangharad. During the 1884-85 season a photograph was taken of the team playing on the Berwyn Ddu Field which lies on the west bank of the river Taff, about a mile north of the town, but two years later the fixture list gives the home venues as the fields at Trallwng and Ynysangharad. As with the playing kit, so with the fields we see evidence of the presence of benefactors. The field at Trallwng was let courtesy of Mr Edwin Phillips, Butcher, until the Central Hotel was built on the site in 1888, and that at Ynysangharad by Mr Gordon Lenox, the employer of Jack Williams at Newbridge Chainworks. Though the modern bandstand now stands on the original playing pitch at Ynysangharad, the club's association with what became Ynysangharad Park was to survive way beyond the events of 1888 and into modern times.

So the players of Pontypridd had a kit, more than one pitch, a club headquarters, and hopefully a sense of togetherness. Matches would be followed by a quick wash under the coldwater tap at the Maltsters' Arms, but they may not have ventured into the bar for a quick beer. There were many temperance societies in the town in the 1880s and some of the players may have been members. They may, instead, have retired to one of the many restaurants in the town. There is no record of this happening, or for that matter anything being done for the visiting team. The visit of a big club such as Newport may have necessitated a special 'bit of a do'.

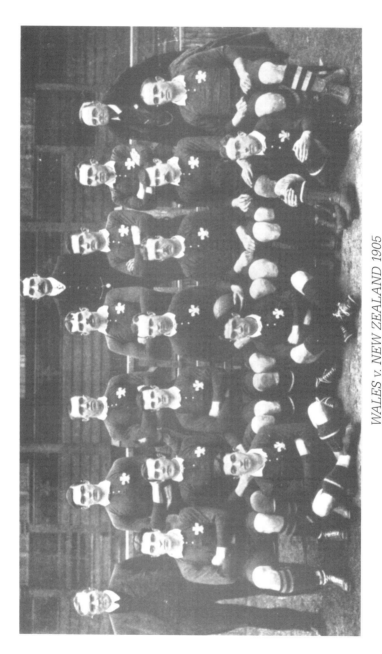

WALES v. NEW ZEALAND 1905

The names are immortal : Bush and Owen, Gwyn Nicholls and Willie Llewellyn, Rhys Gabe, Teddy Morgan and all the other fifteen heroes. Also there, playing their own part in history, are Pontypridd's very own Ack Llewellyn (Back) and Tom Williams (Far left)

A heritage of sorts had already been established by 1888. Years later in his newspaper article of 1926, James Spickett, the club's founder, said

"At that early time the players paid their own expenses, and as far as the Pontypridd club was concerned we had a field free of charge at the spot where the Bandstand is now situated in Ynysangharad Park. And I can remember too that the spectators had their entertainment for nothing for the most part. We might have charged them a small sum on occasions when it was necessary to pay for the use of the field. We had wonderful crowds and we did not fail to give them the exhibition they desired. There is much more commercialism about the game now than existed in my day, and that is what I don't like."

James Spickett was a man of vision. Just as he showed remarkable prescience about the advance of "commercialism" and its effects, so too did the club that his vision had help establish in the 1870s refuse to die for long in 1888. Within a short space of time Pontypridd Rugby Football Club would rise from the ashes,

But that, as they say, is another story.

FOOTNOTE

The writing of this book has been based on contemporary match reports collated by Gareth Harris from the following newspapers -

Barry Dock News
The Carmarthen Journal
The Glamorgan Free Press
The Llanelly and County Guardian
Merthyr Express
Pontypridd Chronicle
Pontypridd Herald
South Wales Daily News
Western Mail

The wider contextual information on rugby in the late 19th century has been gleaned from the published histories of JBG Thomas and Dai Smith and Gareth Williams' inspirational masterpiece, *Fields of Praise*. Invaluable cross-referencing of club records was achieved by consulting CS Arthur's *History and Statistics 1876-1906* which underpins all the later work on Pontypridd's neighbours at Cardiff Rugby Club.

All match reports that were traced have been faithfully reproduced from the original, which accounts for much of the splendidly descriptive terminology. Modern sports' reporting, whether for the broadsheet or tabloid reader, would do well to reflect on some of its Victorian heritage.

Players were not tackled but "collared", which presumably would incur the wrath of the fussy modern referee. The ball was the "oval" or, more commonly, the "leather" which would be "sent into the visitors' territory" or "set in motion". At least one restart from the '25' was described as a "Messer", suggesting a technical deficiency that still afflicts Welsh players today ! If a kick hit an upright, it was a "Poster" and if it succeeded it might be described as the "Trick". A team that was facing defeat might be suffering the "Agony".

More prosaically, some but not all match reports gave team line-ups. Where they did, they have been included as listed at the time. The proportion of backs and forwards underwent a significant change in the late 1880s. The influence of Frank Hancock and the four threequarter system in Cardiff in 1884 is well-documented. Unfortunately, an even greater influence at Pontypridd from time to time was the number of players who turned up; only when they had done a head count could they contemplate a formation.

The scoring system was also undergoing change. Before 1875, all matches were decided on goals alone and tries did not count unless converted into a goal. Early match reports might also refer to a touchdown (or rouge). Then in 1875 the system was changed so that if the number of goals was equal or no goals had been kicked the result could be decided by a majority of tries. The principle of *points* scoring was first introduced in 1886 and a try was counted regardless of the number of goals. A goal counted as three points and a try one point. A side scoring three tries to a goal could therefore draw a match. A try became worth three points in 1893.

Another impression that arises from the match reports is that of indiscipline. Quite apart from the problem of raising teams, of borrowing players, or indeed of turning up on time, several of the matches seem to have had their fair share of mild anarchy. Tries and goals were "disputed", time was wasted in arguments, and teams walked off the field. The two Umpires could disagree amongst themselves, hastening the need for a lone referee.

Perhaps the mood of the time was best summed up by the celebrated rugby writer, "Old Stager" :

"That e'en tho' vanquished,
They could argue still".

Hopefully, the research that Gareth Harris has put into this book will settle many an argument about the early days of Pontypridd Rugby Football Club.

PONTYPRIDD CAPTAINS
1877 - 1888

1877-78	James Spickett
1878-79	Henry Briscoe
1879-80	Unknown
1880-81	David Treharne
1881-82	Unknown
1882-83	James Spickett
1883-84	William Spickett
1884-85	Richard Lewis
1885-86	Eddie Llewellyn
1886-87	Gwilym Lewis
1887-88	William Williams
1888-89	Unknown
1889-90	No team

REPORTED MATCHES

1878-1888

1878

October 24	Aberdare		Away	Drawn
October 26	Monkton House School		Home	Won
November 7	Cardiff Banks		Away	Lost
November 30	10th Glamorganshire Rifle Volunteers		Home	Won

1879

October 16	Cowbridge Grammar School		Home	Won

1880

October 28	Aberdare		Home	Won
November 4	Maindee	*Cup Match at*	*Cardiff*	Won
November 13	Bridgend		Home	Won
December 9	Aberdare		Home	Won

1881

February 12	Cardiff	*Cup Match*	Away	Lost

1882

December 23	Cardiff		Away	Lost

1883

January 11	Merthyr		Away	Lost
January 13	Cardiff		Away	Lost
December 26	Cardiff		Away	Won

1884

January 10	Merthyr *Second XV Match*	Away	Lost
March 6	South Wales University College	Away	Lost
October 25	Llanelli	Away	Lost
November 1	Cardiff	Away	Lost

1885

January 8	Merthyr	Away	Lost
January 8	Merthyr *Second XV Match*	Home	Won
January 18	Merthyr	Away	Lost
February 7	Newport *Cup Match*	Away	Lost
September 26	Newport	Away	Lost
October 3	Cardiff Reserves	Home	Lost
October 24	Mountain Ash	Away	Lost
December 5	Cardiff Reserves	Away	Lost

1886

January 2	Cardiff Reserves	Away	Lost
February 6	Carmarthen *Cup Match at Swansea*		Lost
February 14	Cardiff Harlequins	Home	Won
October 2	Cardiff Harlequins	Away	Drawn
October 9	Newport	Home	Lost
October 23	Penarth	Away	Won
October 30	Maindee	Home	Won
November 4	Old Boys *'A' Team Match*	Home	Won
November 25	Merthyr	Home	Won
December 4	Newport	Away	Lost
December 11	Cardiff Crusaders	Away	Abandoned
December 18	Cardiff Harlequins	Home	Terminated

1887

January 15	Penarth	Home	Drawn
January 29	Merthyr	Away	Won
March 3	Llanelli *Cup Match*	Away	Lost
March 5	Newport	Away	Lost
September 8	Cardiff Harlequins	Home	Lost
September 15	Grangetown	Home	Won
November 5	Newport	Away	Lost
November 10	Merthyr	Away	Postponed
December 24	Penarth	Away	Lost

1888

January 7	Swansea	Away	Lost
March 17	Penarth	Home	Won
September 22	*Cardiff Harlequins' 9-a-Side Tournament*		
November 24	Llandaff	Home	Lost
December 1	Penarth	Away	Lost
December 15	Bridgend	Away	Lost

RUGBY RELICS

61 Leonard Street, Neath, West Glam., SA11 3HW
Tel: 01639 646725 Fax: 01639 638142

The leading supplier of Rugby Memorabilia Worldwide
Featured on BBC, S4C & Radio Wales

New Books for sale:- pp = number of pages

WELSH BREWERS RUGBY ANNUAL FOR WALES	97/8 £5.95, 95/6 £5.45, 91/2 £4, 90/1 £3.50
ROTHMANS RUGBY UNION YEARBOOK	97/8 £16.99, 96/7 £16.99, 95/6 £16.99
WOODEN SPOON/ WHITBREAD RUGBY WORLD ANNUAL	1991 1993 1994 1995 1996 £7.50 each,
1997	£9.99
ROB ANDREW "A Game and a Half" 1994, 186pp, English Outside Half (p/back £6.99)	£14.99
ROB ANDREW "World Cup '95 Diary" 1995, 135pp, paperback	£14.99
GARY ARMSTRONG/DEREK DOUGLAS "Jethart's Here", 224pp, autobiography of Scottish scrum-half	£14.99
STUART BARNES "Smelling of Roses", 1994, 206pp, autobiography of Bath & England outside half	£14.99
BARRIE CORLESS "Rugby Union - The Skills of the Game", 1993, 121pp, coaching book, paperback	£7.99
DOBSON, Paul "Doc - The Life of Danie Craven" 1994, 297pp, biography of "Mr Rugby	£15.00
DOBSON, Paul Chester Williams - A South African Hero", 1996, 64pp, includes free poster	£6.00
DEREK DOUGLAS "The Book of Rugby Quotations" 1991, 287pp, paperback,	£7.99
IEUAN EVANS/PETER JACKSON "Bread of Heaven" 224pp, autobiography of Welsh winger	£14.99
IVAN FALLON "The Player: Tony O'Reilly", Ireland & Lions wing, paperback	£6.99
ROBERT GATE "Gone North Vol 1" 1986, 173pp, Welshmen who have gone to League	£6.50
ROBERT GATE "Gone Vol 2" 1988, 182pp,	£9.90
GUSCOTT/JONES "At The Centre" Jeremy Guscott autobiography	£16.99
FARMER/HANDS "The Tiger's Tale" 1993, 416pp, official history of Leicester	£24.95
HASTINGS/THOMAS "High Balls & Happy Hours", 1994, 192pp, Gavin Hastings autobiography, paperback	£9.99
HASTINGS/DOUGLAS "Great Scott" 1996, 190pp, Scott Hastings autobiography	£14.99
BOB HOLMES/CHRIS THAU "My Greatest Game: Rugby" paperback, 50 stars describe their greatest game	£9.99
D MANSEL JONES "Ystradgynlais Centenary 1890 - 1990", 1991, 220pp	£11.40
STEPHEN JONES "Endless Winter" 2nd ed. 1994, 295pp, updated to include England in SA 94, paperback	£9.99
FRANK KEATING "The Great Number Tens" 1993,, 271pp, an entertaining read, what no Jenkins?	£16.99
LE ROUX, Johan "Biting Back" 1995, 85pp, autobiography of Springbok prop	£7.00
McGEECHAN, Ian "Heroes All" 1997, 140pp, official story of 97 Lions in South Africa	£16.99
PHIL MELLING "Man of Amman" 1994, 135pp, Union player who went North, paperback	£7.95
PROBYN/NEWCOMBE "Upfront", 1993, 191pp, autobiography of English prop forward	£14.99
DAVID PARRY JONES "Action Replay", 1993, 199pp, broadcaster's autobiography, paperback	£9.95
RICHARDS, Dean "Deano" Leicester & England, autobiography	£16.99
ROBERTSON, IAN "Rugby World Cup 1995"	£15.99
RUTHERFORD, Don "Mini Rugby" 1993, 253pp, paperback, coaching	£8.99
SCALLY, John "The Giants of Irish Rugby" 1996, 224pp, 40 player profiles	£14.99
WESTCOTT, Gordon, "A Century on the Rugby Beat" 1993, 212pp, history of rugby in the South Wales Const. area	£10.00
WILLIAMS, Gareth "1905 and All That" 1991, 250pp, sociological study of Welsh Rugby,	£8.75
WILLIAMS, Graham "Code War" 1994, 192pp, early days of Union, League & soccer	£9.95
YORE PUBLICATIONS "Famous Footballers", reprint of rugby photos from 1896 book, limited edition of 250	£25.00

Visa & Mastercard accepted, cheques and postal orders payable to "Rugby Relics", please add £1 postage & packing per book.

Write or ring for our monthly catalogue of Rugby Memorabilia, containing new & secondhand rugby books, programmes, annuals, badges, magazines, autographs, etc.

Collections of Rugby Memorabilia wanted, old programmes, books, caps, photos etc, highest prices paid

RUGBY UNLIMITED

RUGBY UNLIMITED is an independent sports' agency that provides articles, reports and illustrations to the full range of publications and broadcasting outlets throughout the world. It publishes rugby brochures and books of a historical nature and will accept commissions from, or support the research initiatives of, the game's enthusiasts.

The services provided by **RUGBY UNLIMITED** include :

- Articles and illustrations to magazines and programmes
  Personal reminiscences by players and officials
  History of the game (matches, laws, players)
  Player Profiles
  Current news and issues
- Research and background information to both publications and radio and television stations.
- Match reports and reflections to the full range of media outlets.
- The hire of rugby artefacts to organisations wishing to celebrate the history of the game.
- Reviews of new books, videos and other marketed products.
- The printing, publication and marketing of new brochures and books under the **RUGBY UNLIMITED** imprint.

RUGBY UNLIMITED will consider commissions at short notice, as well as medium - and long - term contracts.

FORTHCOMING BOOKS

Spring 1998 "DRAGONS ON TOUR"
A history of all Welsh National Tours overseas since the first to South Africa in 1964 featuring exclusive interviews, personalities and statistics.

Summer 1999 "THE BOOK OF RUGBY MEMORABILIA"
In the year of the World Cup a comprehensive guide to the rich range of·collectables linked to the great game, from pottery to medals, equipment to rare books, as well as programmes and cigarette cards,. Profusely illustrated.

Subscription service available for above titles

CONTACTS -
Dave Richards	*Tel :* 01639 646725	(Overseas + 44 1639 646725)
	Fax: 01639 638142	(Overseas + 44 1639 638142)
Alan Evans	*Tel :* 01827 383067	(Overseas + 44 1827 383067)
	Fax: 01827 383880	(Overseas + 44 1827 383880)

OFFICE ADDRESS - 61 Leonard Street Neath South Wales SA11 3HW